Learning the
Dance of Attachment

**An Adoptive/Foster Parent's Guide
to Nurturing Healthy Development**

By Holly van Gulden
and Charlotte Vick

Published by Holly van Gulden and
Charlotte Vick

Adoptive Family Counseling Center
3338 18th Ave South
Minneapolis, MN 55407

Revised 2010

ISBN 978-0-557-56979-3

90000

9 780557 569793

1

Family

Family is important
it's the main thing
in life
If you don't have
one
it stabs like a
knife

It hurts so bad
It hurts deep inside
And if you look at
yourself
you see no pride

Be a happy person
and live with light
Show a big smile
a smile with
delight

Fight the bad
and fight the pain
Or you will be
living in vain

Love is Powerful

Love is a powerful
work
Love is a powerful
thing
It's your most
valuable part
It's worth more than
a million dollar ring

Love can guide you
from darkness
It can give you light
It's the most
beautiful thing
and it makes your
spirit bright

It's like a clock
but it lasts way
longer
And as I give more
love
my self-image gets
stronger

Love is powerful
Love is love
It's a gift from God
sent from up above

Written by Mariah at age 13, adopted at age 9.

Learning the Dance of Attachment

An Adoptive/Foster Parent's Guide to Nurturing Healthy Development

Forward

Parents routinely take their children for a physical check-up and seek inoculations soon after adoptive placement. *Learning the Dance of Attachment* provides a way for new adoptive and foster parents to complete an emotional development check-up too. If you read this Guide before your child comes home, it provides tips to smooth the transition and helps you set realistic expectations. The *Guide* also helps you assess your own childhood issues and minimize them, so they will not interfere with your parenting skills. After the child comes home, the *Guide* will help you understand normal developmental milestones and highlight behavior that needs special attention or professional help. It also provides the tools you need to enhance your child's ability to attach no matter what age your child was when she joined your family and no matter how long your child has been with you.

This *Guide* has been written to empower adoptive parents. We know that the vast majority of adopted children do well without need for extra help. We also know that adoptive parents are generally wonderful, loving people who are well intentioned. Understanding basic child development and learning certain parenting techniques can help promote healthy attachment. In particular, children adopted at older ages often bring emotional baggage because of early abuse, neglect and lack of healthy attachment. Their maladaptive behaviors often reflect lost or missed developmental experiences. This *Guide* can you help identify problems and find solutions.

A book cannot solve all problems that arise in family relationships—and this *Guide* is no different. If you have concerns, or if your child exhibits extreme symptoms or physically hurtful behavior, seek professional help. Early intervention is always most effective. Don't wait until problems are so severe that you feel like quitting.

Learning the Dance of Attachment: An Adoptive/Foster Parent's Guide for Nurturing Healthy Development is based on the therapy techniques developed by Holly van Gulden and Claude Riedel.

Ms. van Gulden, of Adoptive Family Counseling Center, and co-author of *Real Parents, Real Children,* is an internationally known expert on the needs of adopted children. She is an adoptive parent, sister to adopted children, a family counselor, writer, and lecturer.

Charlotte Vick, the co-writer of the *Guide*, is the former Director of Crossroads Wisconsin office and is also an adoptive parent, social worker and attorney.

Claude Riedel, a psychologist, adopted adult and Co-Director of Adoptive Family Counseling Center, was instrumental in developing the ideas and tools reflected in this book.

Ann Sutton, the former Director of Scottish Adoption, Edinburgh, deserves thanks for her many years of work done to develop and test ways of bringing this work directly to families. Many other people, too numerous to list—staff, parents, and adoption experts—contributed their input to this document. Thank you!

Contents

Section I. The Dance of Attachment - Healthy Development Basics

Human infants learn about the world through relationships with parents. Even in the womb the child hears voices, enjoys movement, and is affected by poor nutrition and drugs or alcohol. The parent-child relationship is essential in helping the child develop positive core perceptions of self. As the science of physical brain development is perfected, it confirms that learning is both emotional and physical. The infant's relationship with the world begins with the physical exploration of the external world (outside of the womb) and culminates in the formation of an internal structure of self.

Attachment is built on stable, reliable, consistent, safe, secure, comfortable, valuing, joyous and loving care. The quality of this relationship is reflected in the child's later capacity to hold permanence and constancy of self and others. Both these capacities form as a result of experiences with consistent caregivers.

Note: In adoption there is some confusion about the term caregiver, it might be defined as birth parent, foster parent, baby sitter, or adoptive parent. In this Guide however, the term parent refers to the person(s) who provide consistent and permanent basic care for the child.

Permanence and **constancy** are two critically essential features of a healthy attachment and a healthy ego. Simply stated, **permanence** means the child's ability to perceive that parents come back even when out of sight and that they continue to exist when out of sensory contact. **Constancy** means the child's ability to <u>feel</u> that the parent's love, safety, comfort, warmth, value and joy are still available—even when the parent is angry, frustrated, disappointed, or irritated. Constancy helps the child maintain a sense of self (as a complex, many faceted person) in the face of frustration. The child understands that this love is also available when she shows negative behaviors.

Attachment between a parent and child is a two-way relationship. While the child or newborn infant is the dependent party in the relationship, parents also have needs, wants, abilities, and limitations. A parent's needs impact his or her ability to build critical connections with the child. As you review these childhood developmental steps, examine your own origins and identify shadows and issues. Self-awareness is an effective tool for helping your child.

Children, even infants, bring to the relationship sensory abilities, perceptions, and limitations that can profoundly influence the growth of attachment. The parents' ability to consistently and reliably meet the biological and psychological needs of the child with comfort and warmth, and the child's ability to receive the parent's offerings, both contribute to the strength or weakness of attachment.

In general, the less unparented time, trauma, neglect, or abuse a child suffers, the easier it is for adoptive parents to help him grow in healthy ways. Older children may have missed more essential developmental steps and tend to bring more baggage—although this is not always true. The good news is that most of these early developmental steps can be (and must be) successfully revisited at later ages if initially missed.

There are several key steps in the normal dance of attachment: 1. A slow Waltz, also called the **Fog** because the infant doesn't realize he is a separate person from his mother. It is a time of touching each other and building safety; 2. The Tango of **Symbiosis**, is a time of learning to fall in love through positive interactions and loving gazes; 3. The Square Dance of **Belonging and Claiming**, I love you no matter what part of you is showing, go away but come back to me; 4. The Tap Dance of **Differentiation**, turning outward and finding a separate self and wanting to dance alone, at least for a little while; 5. The two-step of **Practice,** seeing the world from the floor and then as an upright person; 6. The Hip-Hop of **Rapprochement**, a challenging time of vacillation between separation anxiety and independence; 7. The Ballet of **Individuation** is the time of learning to be an individual and star in the show; and 8. The Clog of **Resiliency**, built on numerous repeat performances.

These steps usually occur around specific ages but depending on circumstances, each individual's timing may differ. Whenever they occur, these steps are essential in building a secure and warm attachment. Each step, even if missed or weakened by parental loss, can be successfully revisited at any age.

Section II. Learning the Dance Steps

We titled this book *Learning the Dance of Attachment* because attachment has both physical and emotional aspects—similar to dance. Also, treatment options for older children replicate the sensory input of the slow Waltz of the fog and the Tango of the symbiotic steps. Most senses—touch, rhythmic movement, hearing, smell, sight, and body position—are engaged. Dance—appropriate for the child's age— builds positive connections.

The dance of attachment between the infant and parent guides the infant from the fog of birth through oneness with the parent and then to a separate self that is safely connected to, protected by, nurtured, and valued by the parent. It is the dance of proximity and exploration. The growing child becomes increasingly free to explore the parent's world.

Attachments are dynamic, not static. They grow, change, and adapt to the changing tasks of the emerging child's, inner self. Attachments flex, and adapt to the changing needs of the two "attached" people throughout life. Children who miss developmental steps for any reason, will have difficulty completing the same steps in later childhood and in their adult relationships unless they have appropriate help. Understanding the stages of attachment formation allows us to assess the quality, strength, and durability of the attachment. It also helps identify developmental work needed in any emotionally intimate relationship. Surprisingly, adult intimate relationships follow the same predictable steps of relationship formation as do parent/infant attachments.

Note to Adoptive/Foster Parents The first part of this book may be somewhat frustrating to read because you'll say to yourself—"We missed that age," or "My child came too late for the symbiosis step." Or "My child came home at age nine and is now a teen-ager. This is not what I need." Reading about it may even make you sad because it evokes the pain of not being with your child at birth. You may wonder why this information is even relevant for you.

However, please persist in your reading because it's essential that parents understand each attachment step. Adoptive parents and therapists often have to revisit earlier stages to repair missed steps which are needed to form the foundation for attachment. You'll need to understand typical behavior to identify and repair problems. More importantly, you'll have fun playing baby games, games of shared laughter, of connection, of attachment with your newly adopted preschooler or child. Engaging in the Dance of Attachment is fun and fun is an extremely important part of parenting!

Nobody Cheered When He Pooped in the Potty David was a beautiful three-year-old when adopted. Despite a four-day transition period of visiting back and forth at the foster home, it was clear that when his new family finally drove home to another state he was apprehensive. David behaved perfectly but showed his fear through his body. It took five days—and a lot of worrying— before he had a bowel movement. It took another nine days at home before he finally had a tantrum. Mom sighed with relief. The physical release and his age appropriate misbehaver demonstrated that he was finally feeling safer. Today David is a well-adjusted and loving adult who makes his parents proud. It was important that his parents were able to identify and respect his fear and revisit some of the earlier steps to strengthen his ability to attach.

Chapter 1. The Slow Waltz (Fog) - Building Safety from Birth to Six Weeks

In the first weeks of life the infant signals its needs by crying. Parents respond to the signal, identify the cause and then meet the dependent infant's needs. Called the need cycle or the arousal/relaxation cycle, this cycle is repeated and completed hundreds of times.

In the first days, weeks, and months of life, the newborn and the new parents are in the fog. The infant's fog is adjusting to the out-of-womb world and becoming physically separate. The parent's fog is learning to read and to interpret the infant's signals, meet the infant's needs, and adjust to this new responsibility. The parent's task is to respond to the child's signals of distress and help the child return to a state of relaxation in a timely manner. It is during the first stage of attachment that trust begins and constancy develops.

Sensory Experience Infants learn about parents and self through the senses. Attachments are originally sensory connections—touch, smell, taste, sound, sight, and the sixth sense, proprioception. (Proprioception, the sixth sense, refers to a combination of body position in space and a sense of movement and rhythm.) At a very elementary level, humans form or pursue relationships when they perceive each other as pleasing to the senses.

The needs cycle is a sensory experience and begins with the child in a state of relaxation. The infant awakens slowly, crying a little. The parent, in response to the infant's signal, is also slightly aroused. As the infant's cries grow louder, signaling full arousal and unmet needs, the parent reaches full arousal, responds to the signal and goes to meet the baby's needs. Touched, dry, full, and burped, the infant returns to a state of contentment and full relaxation. The healthy newborn learns that he or she can signal the parent and receive care. It is imperative that the cycle is complete most of the time. If either the infant or the parent is unable to relax on a repetitive basis, the infant experiences the world as uncomfortable and unreliable. **The needs cycle builds the foundation of trust and security for the infant.**

<u>Molding</u> Newborn infants have little or no ability to hold up any part of their bodies. The infant's body "molds" to the parent's body as it is being held. Newborns are like jelly, they settle into the parent's arms when they are in the state of full relaxation or homeostasis. (Homeostasis—means a relatively stable state of equilibrium. All living things seek to maintain a constant internal environment.) Infants who do not feel safe and comforted in the parent's arms often arch away from the parent or turn their heads away, avoiding contact, unable to relax with the parent. **One of the signs that the parent and the infant are connecting on a sensory level is the way the infant's body relaxes in the parent's arms.**

During the Waltz or fog stage, the infant experiences safety, comfort and warmth over and over and over. In sensory contact with the parents the distressed infant returns to that state of molded bliss; safety, comfort and warmth. These are the first life experiences outside the womb which provide sensory and emotional calming. In the parent's arms the child goes from a state of agitation to calm.

The sensory presentation of the new caregiver can affect the child's ability to relax. No two caregivers look, smell, touch, taste, sound, or move in exactly the same way. For some

14

children sensory differences are very important. The child may not be able to relax in the arms of the new parent because they sound, taste, and smell unfamiliar. Sensory disconnects (the child's inability to <u>feel</u> the comfort offered by the caregiver) happen more often after a child has had multiple caregivers but can also occur with infant adoptions or birth children. A child's illness, brain defects, an immature sensory system or inability to adjust to the sensory input of a parent can hinder attachment. Also, too many primary caregivers can impair an infant's capacity to experience safety, security, comfort, and warmth offered in a new family.

The parent's own unconscious emotional issues can also inhibit the process. A parent's unresolved grief, depression, physical illness, and unmet needs from childhood are just a few of the possible factors that may complicate his or her ability to relax with his or her child. A parent's frustration, anger and concern about a child's or teenager's repetitive inappropriate behavior can inhibit a parent's ability and desire to mold with the child.

If either the parent or the infant is unable to relax in sensory contact with each other, the cycle is not complete.

I'm too Angry to Hug You Sara joined her family through adoption when she was nine years old. At first, hugs were stiff and she only hugged on her terms. Over time she relaxed and even learned to give semi-molded hugs at her parents' request. Mom and Dad were pleased.

When Sara had been home a few years she began lying and blaming her brother for her bad behavior. No matter what the consequences, Sara continued to lie. Her parents were angry and confused. One night after a particularly difficult day, Sara came and asked if Mom was going to tuck her in and give her a hug. Mom responded, "I'm too angry, why would I want to hug you?" Sara began to shake and left the room. She returned an hour later with a packed suitcase. "When do I leave?" She asked. Sara's mom said, "I'm angry but you are not leaving, Why would you think you are leaving?"

"Because," Sara answered, "for a long time now you have been teaching me to hug. I've been hugging like I used to and now you won't hug me at all."

Sara's mom was shocked. She gave Sara a big molded hug and called Holly the next day. Holly helped Sara's mom understand the lying as a missed developmental step. Sara's parents learned to discipline and maintain the sensory connection—they learned again to mold.

In Adoption It's possible and very important to look at parent/child interactions for signs that the arousal/relaxation/molding step has been successfully completed. Some children—such as those who experience neglect, abuse, frequent moves, or are emotionally or physically disconnected, and those who have medical or emotional conditions, which inhibit the development of a sense of safety and security—never form that critical sense of trust with the first caregivers. However, attachment can still be enhanced in the relationship no matter how long the parent and child have been together or how they came together.

Adoptive parents need to overcome the child's early maladaptive lessons. What's outside, an unsafe and unpredictable world goes inside: "The world is not safe, I am not safe. The world is unreliable, I'm unreliable."

Chapter 2. Dancing the Tango (Symbiosis) Positive Interactions and Falling in Love from Four Weeks to Five Months

By the fourth or fifth week of life, the arousal/relaxation cycle has been repeated hundreds of times and trust has developed. One afternoon the parent leans over the crib and smiles at the baby as she has so many times before. This time is different. This time the baby smiles. Mom smiles back at the baby who is smiling at her. **Wow, what a feeling!**

This is the first positive interaction and the first "mirroring game." Mirroring games are crucial developmental steps of human development. They create a mutual experience of sensory connectedness, shared joy, value, and reciprocity.

At this age the child has no sense of permanence.

Gas—or Not? Four week-old baby Lisa is clearly the most beautiful girl in the world. She has large hazel eyes and curly brown hair and loves to snuggle. One day as dad was changing her diaper she gifted him with a broad smile. His heart immediately melted and he called his mom—Lisa's grandmother—to brag. "She smiled at me," he exclaimed, "She knows that I'm her daddy, she never smiles at anyone else." Grandma congratulated him, laughed to herself and thought, "It's just gas." However, to dad and baby it was joyous connection.

Any part of self or the parent not currently felt or sensed does not exist. A baby gazing at the light waves his hand into line of sight and for few seconds the hand exists. When the hand flops onto the mattress out of sight it no longer exists.

In these first months there are two main patterns of healthy parenting to nurture permanence and they are: 1. limiting the number of caregivers—to help the child identify primary caregivers, and 2. sensory overlap. Sensory overlap means that dads (or moms) big voice, face, etc. are all associated with comfort. When dad holds the baby he looks at the baby, moves his head away while still touching the baby. The baby learns from experience that if daddy's love is still there his face (head) will come back. This is sensory overlap. The child should be bathed in many forms of sensory connections. Utilize all senses—songs for hearing, massage and warmth for touch, comforting smells, happy faces for sight, and repetitive motions—all over and over again.

Baby and parents are beginning to share joy, to experience comfort, value, and warmth with each other. This is the interactive step of the dance of attachment called the tango of positive interactions. Parent and child are falling in love. They smile and they gaze into one another's eyes. At this step of the relationship development, parents begin to call the baby by his or her name. They use cute nicknames and they focus a great deal of attention on their baby. The play peek-a-boo and give nose kisses.

Intimate Eye Contact Symbiosis between an infant and parent usually begins with the first interactive smile. One of the features of the first interactive smile is the eye-to-eye contact that accompanies the exchange of smiles. As parent and infant repeat the exchanges of smiles, they become entranced with each other. Eye contact that started as part of the joyous exchange of smiles becomes a positive interaction. Simple tools such as a stroller that faces the parent to enhance eye contact or a baby carrier that facilitates touch can help build attachment.

Early in the symbiotic stage of attachment, the parent and infant hold the gaze for two to five seconds, but as their relationship strengthens, the gaze lengthens. By the end of the symbiotic stage, parent and infant hold their gaze for as long as 10 to 20 seconds. Increasing the length of the symbiotic gaze is a sign of healthy symbiosis.

As eye contact lengthens it also becomes more intense. By the fifth month, parent and child show the capacity to return to the gaze even if something startles them. This rejoining phenomenon demonstrates the strength of the connection. **Avoidance of eye contact is common with children who have missed or had symbiosis interrupted by changes in caregivers.**

Comfort, Joy, and Value A parent's main task during this stage is to nurture the infant/parent connection, to add sensory experiences of joy, value, and love to the ongoing process of protecting and meeting the infant's needs. This task begins during the Fog Step and continues throughout childhood. The parent must nurture the infant and fall in love without projecting his or her own needs as the infant's needs. This boundary between self and the child is difficult for the parent to maintain in the symbiotic stage.

During the symbiotic stage, interactions should not be based on the child's performance. The child does not have to achieve or perform to earn loving responses. The parent smiles and gazes because the parent values the baby, just for being. **What's outside goes inside.** The joy and value experienced in relation to the parent goes inside to form a crucial part of the child's healthy self. Child and parent can bring joy to each other and can experience joy in each other.

The shared experience of brief positive interaction is the cement that emotionally binds the caregiver and child.

Like the intimate eye gazing of this stage and of adults in loving relationships, positive inter-actions are brief, lasting seconds not minutes. While the actual "touching" with a wink, a gaze, or a smile is brief, the effects can last a long time and can be recalled days and years later. This is the shared joy of life. It is the first experience of intimacy.

Toward the end of the symbiotic period, as attachment progresses, the theme becomes a tug-of-war between symbiosis and separateness. The intense experience of connection, the celebration of one's existence though multiple positive interactions, lays the groundwork for healthy growth.

In Adoption The dance of attachment between a parent and a newly adopted child who is not an infant (or between two adults prior to marriage), develops from the fog of two separate "individuals" meeting and learning each other's cues. In this situation they strive to create a connection without losing their separate "identities". At the beginning of the symbiotic step of any relationship moving towards intimacy, the two individuals in the relationship focus most of their energy and attention on each other and their "union". Boundaries between self and another at this stage can become blurred or lost as the two build a unit. An adult with deficits in permanence is at risk of engulfing or consuming the other person. That person becomes enmeshed in symbiosis and unconsciously attempts to hold the other partner in this state and stage, consuming the other's separateness or losing their own identity in the other person. Other people have "commitment issues." These people with deficits in permanence leave or run from symbiosis before the relationship is strong enough to weather the distance. Older adopted children without permanence have sometimes been described as "pushing people away" or "consuming all my attention." These behaviors demonstrate missed steps.

Chapter 3. The Square Dance (Belonging and Claiming) – Expressing Love and Fostering Connections, from Birth to Adulthood

All humans need to feel that they belong in their families and that their family claims them.   Belonging/claiming is a cornerstone of healthy attachment. Human beings are social and the need to belong is as fundamental as the need for touch. As they grow, children must experience a warm and secure connection to parents. Belonging and claiming activities start in early infancy and must continue throughout childhood.

Belonging and claiming activities resemble a square dance. Sometimes people dance as partners, then they separate as they do-se-do and ultimately come back together. Occasionally dancers change partners for a while. There are specific steps to be learned and one must always stay in rhythm with the music. The more one dances the more confident the dancer becomes.   Dancing partners and "squares" attach and become fast friends.

The tools for claiming are many, including statements such as: 1. my beautiful baby, 2. you are my daughter and I love you, 3. wow, that's my girl, 4. you must get your music ability from me, 5. your smiling face belongs in our family, and 6. keep swimming, I'll be your cheerleader.

A child's sense of belonging is reflected when you hear him say: I'm a football player like you, our family sure is funny, and we all need to help Aunt Beth with our new cousin.

It seems like this square dance should be easy but an angry child can make it very difficult to find things to compliment or claim. At times you'd rather keep walking away in the do-de-do than return as the child needs. In turn, a parent focused on biological appearances might miss positive connections based on behavior not looks. The utilization of "parts" language is one way to help a difficult child see positives and find connections with family.

The Many Parts of Self To belong is to experience that the sum of your "parts" is okay, that all of you is accepted—even though some "parts" of you are not appreciated. To belong securely is to "know" that even if and when the negative parts of self (anger or tantrum) are present, the parent (and the self) will remain constant, stable, and secure.

Most people have parts of themselves that they unconsciously and consciously hide from themselves and others. Belonging is the belief that membership or connectedness will tolerate knowing the hidden parts. The child comes to realize that if my parent accepts all of me, then I can accept all of me. This is an extremely important concept—one that is easily incorporated into daily life. Utilizing "parts" language is one of the most effective tools a parent can have. Check out the section on parts of self later in this book.

What's Outside Goes Inside *Object relations theory hypothesizes that people develop their sense of themselves in the world, through their experiences (and their perceptions of those experiences) with their primary caregivers (seen as objects).*

All of the people below lost someone important. Each of them has symptoms that suggest vulnerability in their internal sense of self; an inability to internally comfort themselves in the face of changes and challenges in their environment. They each lack a stable (and resilient) sense of self.

- *Susan, a 26 year old who joined her family through adoption, says she shatters when a friend criticizes her.*
- *Ramon, a 10 year old, adopted at the age of two, explodes when his parents say "no."*
- *Two-year-old Anna won't allow her parents to hold her even after 11 months.*
- *John's father died when he was 5. John can't sleep without the lights on and the family dog in his bed.*

Keep reading to learn about more tools to help a child establish a firm sense of self and to enjoy the feeling of being claimed and loved.

You Left Me	
You left me alone alone in the dark I'm feeling real sad while I'm here in the park	Just go away you've annoyed me all day I'm not feeling happy I'm feeling real snappy
I'm so very down I'm not so happy Don't come near cause I'll be real snappy	Don't come near or else you will fear I think I'm sad but I'm also mad
I can't take this pain I'm going insane Leave me alone I'm on the phone	Mariah, age 13, wrote this poem about losing her mother when she was age 9.

Chapter 4. The Tap Dance of (Differentiation) Turning Outward and Exploring the Possibility of Separateness, from Five to Nine months

Differentiation is the stage where the infant begins to discover that self and mother may not be one and the same. Two important behaviors demonstrate this new process: (1) visual, manual, and tactile exploration of the parent's face and body and (2) checking. It is a time of bouncing, jumping, wiggling, and head turning—a tap dance on your lap.

During the Fog, infants are cradled in the parent's arms at chest height or cuddled into the mom's shoulder. The infant's face is usually turned towards the source of nourishment, the breast. Around the beginning of the fifth month of life, infant/parent posture adds yet another new dimension; The baby begins to sit on her mom's lap or straddles her hip.

The baby is beginning to explore the parent's world. The pleasurable sensations of the symbiotic step have been enjoyed and savored for several months. Baby and parent have come to anticipate and to begin to "hold" these precious feelings between episodes. Secure and warm in the "holding" of the parent, the infant begins to show an interest in the world outside the perceived oneness of the self/mother. Awake for longer periods of time, five-month-old babies are alert and curious, looking around and exploring the world from the safety of the parent's lap.

<u>Object Permanence</u> **Babies in this age group are learning that <u>objects</u> (parents) continue to exist even when out of sensory contact.** However, babies at this age cannot "hold" the knowledge that the parent exists out of sight, as they have not yet developed evocative object permanence. Babies need **transitional objects** (blankets, teddy or pacifier) to soothe the anxiety they feel when they are "out of touch" with the caregiver. Transitional objects evoke sensory responses that mirror the baby's experience of safety, security, comfort, and warmth when the parent "holds" them. Holding, smelling, rubbing, and tasting the transitional object helps to soothe the baby's anxiety.

<u>Transitional Objects</u> In the stage of differentiation, transitional objects (blankies, thumbs, etc.) are essential to practice attachment formation. Until the toddler can "hold" the parent's existence, she depends on sensory reminders of the transitional object to ease the anxiety of being out there without the parent. Transitional objects also help the child to develop the capacity to self soothe and to tolerate low levels of anxiety. The sight, feel, smell, and taste of the transitional object evokes the comfort and relief from distress that the parent offers when he or she is available. The transitional object will slowly be discarded as the child internalizes permanence and constancy, and learns to feel safe and whole in varying situations. The capacity to ease anxiety and to self-soothe are important precursors to the capacity to delay gratification.

Transitional objects must be durable and readily available. Transitional objects should evoke a "sensory memory" of the parent. They are not always material objects. A song, a phrase, lines from a poem can evoke the safety, security, comfort, and warmth that the individual needs. Adults too, often respond to and find comfort from these non-material types of objects. Symbolic items can also evoke the security of an absent significant other. Wedding rings are symbolic representations of the love and commitment between husband and wife. When there is discord between them, many people unconsciously twist or rub their wedding ring, evoking the memory of the availability of the nurturing, loving partner.

Disappearing Objects - Out of Sight, Out of Mind
Aaron was a boy of six who had not yet developed object permanence. The therapist was using a toy turtle to help him understand that objects can go away and become invisible but still exist. In Aaron's early experience, things or people that left never came back.

She showed him the toy puppet, used it to have a conversation with him. She pulled the turtle's head in and out and finally leaving it in asked him where the turtle had gone. He didn't know. She explained that the turtle was still there but he disagreed. In fact, he became very angry when she insisted that the turtle's head was inside the shell. He was determined that she was wrong and argued and fought to prove himself right. He was so insistent that he was out of control.

It took many repetitions in and out of sight, plus peek-a-boo to help him learn that objects (and people) don't simply disappear.

Checking As the foundations for representational permanence are repeated over and over in the fog and symbiotic steps, the five to seven month old baby can remember the look and feel of the parent. Consider what happens if the baby is sitting on the mom's lap when grandma arrives. Mom hands the baby

27

over to grandma as they have done many times before. This time, the baby stares at mom then at grandma and back at mom again. The baby is realizing in a new way that grandmother is not the mother. As differentiation begins, the baby only stares at the mother. Soon the baby stares at mom, then back at grandma and then mom again. Baby looks to mom for reassurance. Mother smiles and encourages the baby to go to Grandma. Checking is a crucial development; it demonstrates that the child is beginning to localize safety and security in the parent. Checking behavior also demonstrates that the baby is starting to "hold" the parent's image for a few seconds. It's a sign of the child's connection to the parent. People check with their children and their partners throughout life. Young children connect with their parents when they are approaching new experiences. The toddler looks to the parent for reassurance when she goes to pet the goat at the children's zoo.

By the seventh or eighth month, the baby has separation anxiety; exhibiting moderate to strong distress when handed to or left with a stranger. This usual behavior is actually powerful evidence of the developing attachment to the parent.

Contact Needed James joined his family by adoption when he was 9 years old. One year later James' father attended a training by Holly and realized his son often needed to check in. He began bobbing his head around. He was thinking about how he calls out to his son when separating or when James tries new things or when they have been apart for awhile. On one occasion James really had a melt-down at a game. A few months later, James told his dad, "Papa you forgot to nod at me when the soccer game started, that's why I lost it."

The Steps of Attachment and the Impact

Developmental Steps	Typical Developmental Needs	Healthy Parent-Child Interaction	Normal Behavior
Birth to 6 Weeks, Waltz The Fog	Needs safety, and security. Is dependent and must trust in others. Child needs to mold to mom and has a sense of oneness with the parent.	Parents must be available to the child "on demand."	Child cries to signal needs, needs are met, and the child and parent returns to relaxed state of sensory contact with each other.

Accepts cuddling. |
| Early 2-5 months, the Tango Symbiosis | The child needs to fall in love. Thumb sucking, blankies, (transitional objects) evoke a sense of parent's presence. | Parents must psychologically attach to the child, give stimulation, initiate positive interactions, and feel good when together. | Child prefers one caregiver.

A symbiotic (child and parent respond to each other) relationship develops. Parent and child feel as one. |
| Late 5-9 months the Tap Dance, Differentiation | The child needs to learn that self is different from mom, knows strangers are not parents. | "Natural" behaviors such as peek-a-boo, funny faces and coos promote connection. | Child smiles, makes eye contact, vocalizes, watches parent.

Explores parents' faces, pulls, pokes and grabs parents.

Checking out others 'behavior.

Protests absence of caregiver. |

# of Negligent/Inappropriate Experiences-Chart

Inappropriate/ Negative Experiences Affecting the Child	Resulting Behavior	Best New Parental Response
Parent is inconsistent and unpredictable. Child's cries for help are ignored. Parent doesn't like the child, is remote or looks to the child to provide love, and nurturance.	Extreme neglect can endanger the baby's life. • Apathy, socially unresponsive • Failure to thrive • Disinterest in the environment • Chronic sleeping or eating problems • Difficulty settling down, becoming regulated or calm. • Fussy and hard to comfort • Avoidance of physical contact and contact after separation • Hard to settle into a pattern • Disassociation or disconnect	Funnel the child. Don't pass her around to friends even for a little time; limit the number of caregivers so child learns to attach. Loving eye contact, games, play, peek-a-boo, gentle touch. Consistent, kind and gentle responses. Show joy in one-to-one interactions.
The parent is unpredictable—sometimes angry, sad, distant and sometimes loving. The child doesn't feel safe. Child is physically or sexually abused.	Note: older children whose needs haven't been met at this stage may behave as follows: • Lose things-homework after its completed, jackets, socks, and even "special objects" because out-of-sight is out-of-mind. • Wet or mess themselves, day and/or night. • Have difficulty falling asleep • Have difficulty sitting still	Respond appropriately to the child's full range of emotions. Gently calmly and firmly corrects the child and sets boundaries when child hurts others or self. The parent offers nurturing and affirming attachment immediately after corrections.

Chapter 5. Dancing the Two-Step (Practicing) Getting the Feel of Being Apart yet Safely Connected, From Nine to 18 Months

The practicing step entails repetitive experiences of being different from, being away from, and yet safely connected to the parent. Differentiation means beginning to experience and feel the difference between self and others. Practicing is divided in two stages: early (nine to 13 months—the world from the floor) and late (13 to 18 months) upright mobility practicing.

Early Practicing This step is exploring the world from the floor at approximately nine – thirteen months. Crawling marks the beginning of the practicing stage of attachment. The baby's ability to move away from the parent allows him to experience being different and separate from the parent in a whole new way; self-propelled. The baby usually crawls away from the mom, towards the dad. Father and baby have also experienced the fog and developed a symbiotic closeness. The baby perceives the dad as safe, secure, warm, and comforting. Crawling away from proximity with the mom towards proximity with the dad creates a safe environment to explore.

When babies crawl from one caregiver towards another, they check with the mom more frequently, looking back over their shoulders, catching mother's eye and receiving a reassuring nod and smile. They then crawl just a little further away. Checking has become a way of visually re-experiencing the safety, security, and comfort provided by the caregiver.

31

Permanence At around ten months a child will drop a toy off the high chair, reach for it, grunt and gesture. Dad picks it up and almost immediately the child drops it again. He's testing to see if the toy is still there and as it's returned he reacts with joy. Dad has just confirmed for the child that objects continue to exist even when out of sight. The fetch game also helps build the child's experience of things going away and still existing—learning that items and people still exist and come back. This develops the child's sense of permanence. All permanence grows from experiences with parents. Permanence develops first with non-important objects and then transfers to people. The ability to hold permanence means the child takes it for granted that objects (especially parents) will reappear. If a parent has never suffered from a lack of permanence, it's hard to understand this concept. People with permanence generally perceive the world as safe—People without permanence generally perceive the world as unsafe.

Hiding in Plain Sight Little 18-month-old Scot loves to play hide and seek. He looks at mom, squeals and runs to hide, just waiting for her to find him. His favorite hiding place is behind the drapes—the sheer drapes.

Refueling Babies of this age maintain their sense of connectedness, yet spend more and more time further away from their parents. The ability to "hold" the parent's safety with just a visual check is limited. Babies need to refuel by returning to the parent's side for hugs or call the parent to them for hugs by signaling distress. After a brief refuel, the baby has the capacity to crawl away again to safely explore the world at a slight distance from the mother or father.

Late Practicing Exploring the world from an upright position happens at approximately 13-16 months. Late practicing begins as the baby stands up and walks away from the mom. As the baby stands up and walks away, she takes a huge step towards becoming a separate person. Every day, every waking hour the baby gets up and walks away from and then back towards either parent, practicing being separate yet staying connected.

Family Tree Jason, age three years, loves everything about playing peek-a-boo and hiding games. One of his favorites is to assign his father a place to hide. When they go on walks he tells his father to go ahead and hide behind a certain tree. Then when he and his mother catch up he "discovers" his father behind the tree—still there, still available for love and laughter. Jason's game confirms his feeling that, "if I hide you there I can still find you there."

Shadowing and Darting This game reinforces emerging evocative object permanence. This is the ability to hold that important objects—including parents, continue to exist. Toddlers normally begin to develop the capacity to "hold" or remember the existence of the transitional object or person. This allows them to continue exploring and feel safe.

Toddlers love being chased by their parents. Set a toddler down at the park or in the yard and he will dart away, looking back over his shoulder, enticing the parent to give chase. When the parent catches him and scoops him up, the young explorer laughs and laughs, wiggles down and darts off again. This game allows the toddler to experience the power of moving away, be an independent self, and operate under his own steam, coupled with the ability to draw the parent to him, to keep the connection. The parent is quickly available to the child even as the child leaves contact. The child enjoys and delights in darting but sometimes resists being close, refusing hugs and rejecting comfort. This refusal is simply a temporary act to show the child's independence—it should pass very quickly.

> **Shadowing and Darting**   Little 20-month-old James was thrilled to be with the family at his big brother's football game.   Everyone was sitting on blankets on the sideline watching the game.   James soon became bored just sitting with no one paying much attention to him.
>
> About 20 feet away there was a big, beautiful pine tree. He got up and edged toward it—watching mom all the way. Soon he ducked behind, disappearing from view.   Several adult heads turned to watch but wisely refrained from getting suckered into playing the chase game.   Within a minute he peeked out and mom checked in with a wave.
>
> He darted back, waited longer, and then peeked again with a huge smile that said, "catch me if you can."   After about twenty minutes of the hide and peek game, mom sneaked up on him, grabbed him with hugs and kisses. This resulted in peals of laughter and squealing.   Both mom and child reaffirmed connections and had fun.

The Thrill of Self-Esteem Toddlers must want to move away from the parent and explore, otherwise, they tend to avoid experiences that promote independence. Toddlers must receive a great deal of encouragement to practice being different: encouragement to crawl, walk, speak, play, explore, and be curious.

Baby toddles from one side of the room to the other. Concentrating hard and grinning, he falls into dad's arms to cheers, claps, and laughs. This joyous celebration provides

34

external incentive to the internal drive to explore. It's a critical component of the practicing stage; parents must allow, support, and encourage—with sincere delight—the toddler's journeys, efforts, and accomplishments. Joy for effort encourages the child to try and try again. Even that highly irritating stage when the child runs away must be handled with firm, loving, correction—never spanking.

In Adoption Adults adopted as children who had missed experiencing the practicing stage often find it difficult to encourage their partners or children to learn independence. They fear loss of closeness, love, and connection because they do not yet feel sufficient permanence in the relationship or in themselves.

Children who missed healthy fog and symbiosis stages come into their new families with a potentially dysfunctional sense of differentiation. They know that they are separate, but the separation process was not healthy. They differentiated too early. Now, at this point later in their lives, they may either try to control others in a relationship or they totally resist closeness. Reactive Attachment Disorder is the name given when a child so fears loss that she resists or sabotages the relationship. This person fears and resists intimacy as much or more than the practicing toddler fears separation.

The Steps of Attachment and the Impact

Developmental Steps	Typical Developmental Needs	Healthy Parent-Child Interaction	Normal Behavior
The Two-Step of Practicing 9 -18 months Each child learns the difference between parent and self.	Children need a stable, available, nurturing caregiver. Parents must be "safe haven" from which the child can venture out safely and return. Children need consistent and gentle redirection not a parent who overreacts. The parent should gently correct the child and support both individuation and connectedness.	Primary parental relationships are the foundation for all future relation-ships. The child is gradually more social and psychologically separate from parents and increasingly able to explore. The child's intoxicated with newfound mobility, but anxious and apprehensive about physical separateness from the parent. Parents must cheer efforts.	Increasingly social Expanding interest in others Crawls away Emotionally "refuels" by going back to parent Accepts comfort most of the time Increases self - comforting skills by using transitional objects Mimics and models others Is assertive, self-directed, defiant, easily frustrated an. Joyous at accomplishments

# of Negligent/Inappropriate Experiences-Chart

Inappropriate/ Negative Experiences Affecting the Child	Resulting Behavior	Best New Parental Response
The caretaker withdraws support in response to the child's developing separation. This threatens the child's need to take steps toward independence. A child who does not have safe places in which to explore or is abused for venturing out, will be fearful or angry. Physical or sexual abuse. The child loses a parent because of death or adoption. The child is raised in an orphanage setting and/or with multiple caregivers.	Abusive or negligent treatment often results in: • Lack of interest in exploration. • Clinging, fearful behavior • Conversely, absence of stranger anxiety. • Gives affection indiscriminately –always seems to be looking for love or attention. • Inability to be soothed, comforted or nurtured. • Scant or delayed language development. • Greatly vacillating behavior- doesn't feel safe. An older child may exhibit some of the following behaviors: • Impulsive, can't delay gratification. • Takes objects. • Angry outbursts. • Hoarding of food. A child's "selective amnesia" may be real. Memory is affected by past trauma and fear.	Consistent, kind and gentle responses. Funnel the child, Don't pass her around to friends even for a little time; limit number of caregivers so child learns to attach. **This is extremely important!** Loving eye contact, games, play, gentle touch. When child changes behavior, celebrate, say "good job". Redirection, never corporal punishment. Repeat some of the behaviors you would do with a younger child. Play peek-a-boo, hide and seek, etc.

Chapter 6. Dance Hip Hop (Rapprochement) Vacillation Between Dependent Behaviors and Independence, 18-36 months

Parents typically complain about the "terrible twos" and toilet training and running away. If ever a dance provided an apt description of a child's behavior at this age, it would be Hip Hop. Your child, like the dance, is loud, wiggly, jumpy, happy, crabby, up and down, and clingy or rejecting, all with no particular plan, but with great joy in life.

Psychologically, between the ages of 15 and 18 months the child has developed permanence about non-important items. A toy rolls out of sight and the child seeks it. This development continues over the next months and the child develops stronger and stronger permanence about his parents also. He feels they still exist but uses transitional objects (blankies, pacifiers) to reinforce memory of their existence. The child also frequently checks in and refuels his sensory memory links. Permanence is sensory knowledge, not intellectual cognitive knowledge. The baby <u>feels</u> that his parents continue to exist.

Just as mom and dad are becoming comfortable with the toddler's dawning independence, another change occurs. The child feels, "Uh oh, we really are two separate people. How dare you leave me, I want the safety of symbiosis back."

<u>Return of Dependent Behaviors and Anxiety at Separation</u>
The same child who escaped the parent now pursues her, hanging on, exhibiting anxiety and distress when the mother is not available. Many parents find this switch from the chase me game to "do not leave me," distressing. It is very confusing when the toddler displays both behaviors in the same day,

morning, and hour. This vacillation between bidding for, and practicing independence versus seeking return to oneness, is the hallmark of the rapprochement stage. Toddlers in rapprochement can manage some experiences of separateness and fall apart in others.

Wooing the Parent Back The toddler's budding capacity to know that mom and dad still exist even when he cannot see, hear, or touch them can be overwhelmed by the dawning reality that the self exists separately from the parent. Toddlers experiencing rapprochement often want to return to the safety, security, comfort, and warmth of symbiosis, a sense of oneness with the parent. Remember, the older adopted child often behaves as a younger child.

Dead and Gone Sara, age eight. had a very hard day at school. She began crying big tears and would not be comforted. Eventually the principal told Sara her mommy was coming to get her and they would all discuss why Sara was so sad. When Sara's mother arrived, Sara was visibly shocked. She ran to her, grabbed her around the thighs and said, "you aren't dead now!" Sara's mom was horrified, and said, "Sara, I wasn't dead, you know I was at work." Sara, replied, "Oh, I know you go to work mommy but you die and then you get undead. Today I thought you wouldn't get undead and be my mommy again." Sara intellectually knew her mother existed. She could not and did not feel that her mother existed when they were apart. Sara lacked parental permanence.

In Adoption Attachments are not full and complete until all developmental steps are in place and strong and flexible. Constancy—the knowledge that parents are stable people whose nurturance is available even if and when there is tension—is the glue that holds the relationship together. Unfortunately, many relationships lose their constancy during rapprochement. Each individual reacts to the coercive behaviors of the other, moving further and further apart, distanced by tension and misunderstanding, unable to re-establish the safety, security, comfort, and warmth of their union, unable to nurture each other in the relationship.

In adoption parents often tell their children, "We are your forever parents," trying to help the children feel safe. Forever is an abstract, intellectual word. The child can know intellectually his parents exist and yet feel and act as if they are gone forever.

The rapprochement stage is normally repeated in adolescence. If a child is older when adopted and the parent works hard on attachment, he will eventually progress to the rapprochement stage—but the child won't be a cute two-year-old. It may seem odd, but it is a sign of attachment when your 8-year-old in rapprochement whips rapidly between clinging and rejecting.

The Steps of Attachment and the Impact

Developmental Steps	Typical Developmental Needs	Healthy Parent-Child Interaction	Normal Behavior
The Hip-Hop of Rapprochement 18-36 months	Toddlers need to resolve the pull between independence and regression to the dependency of a baby. They need to practice "coming and going" from parents, able to return and "refuel" and separate again. The child needs consistent boundaries and expectations. Rules/boundaries provide security.	The healthy parent stays emotionally available, despite toddler's coming and going. She is there for refueling, then sets the child "free", with assurance, support, and joy. She redirects the child when he does something naughty. The child looks back and grins when "being bad".	Shadowing and darting, child plays hide-and-seek and chase games, Imitating the dance of closeness and separateness. Vacillate between, dependency and autonomy. Oppositional, defiant, stubborn, aggressive, and egocentric. Loves the word no. Moodiness, gets attention from negative behavior. Can tolerate brief separations from caregivers.

Inappropriate/ Negative Experiences Affecting the Child	Resulting Behavior	Best New Parental Response
Harshness or punitive parenting leads to an antagonistic relationship. When neglect or negative attention is the only care available the child, he will settle for negative attention. Over protection teaches child the "danger" of separateness and promotes an ambivalent relationship.	A harmed child will show the typically trying behavior of rapprochement, plus: • Varying behaviors in intensity and frequency depending on the type and severity of neglect or abuse. • Disinterest in play. • Depression and lethargy. • Constant power struggles with unending demands for attention. • Prolonged clinging. • Inappropriate friendliness with others. • Constant attention seeking. • Tantrums Older child • Worse tantrums. • Lying. • Stealing. A child's "selective amnesia" may be real. Memory is affected by past trauma and fear.	Consistent refueling and love. Calm and soft voice responses to misbehavior. Consistent but kind redirecting. Consequences might be time-out chair in sight of parent – one minute per year of age. Don't give in to tantrums- repeat the word no and give a time out. Don't scold, smack, shout, or withhold affection. Encourage individuation and praise accomplishments. See Chapter 13 for additional advice.

Chapter 7.The Ballet Begins (Consolidation of Individuation) - Building the Child's Capacity to "Hold" and Feel the Constancy of the Parent Even When Apart, from 36-54 Months

As rapprochement resolves, the child learns that she is truly not one with the parent. She experiences herself as separate from, yet safely attached. Successful consolidation means the creation of two whole people bonded by trust.

By now, the child understands and feels that mom and dad still exist when they are separated by time, and space. This means she has developed permanence. When the child also understands that the parent's love exists despite changing emotions—anger, sadness, joy, etc.—this means she has developed constancy. By age three, the child has just begun to develop representational and evocative constancy (this means the ability to use soothing objects and/or the ability to remind ones self of the parents constancy). However, tough situations and internal distress can overwhelm this new capacity. The child falls back to earlier behaviors. When this happens, it's good to help your child check-in and refuel.

Typical Adoption Scare
Bette's daughter when in trouble at age three yelled "I want my other mom." Feeling rejected, mom called a friend and was reminded that Ella didn't want birth mom, she wanted loving mom.
Bette went back, offered to read a book. Ella sighed and said, "that's what I wanted—Mommy!"

Allow him to use objects to "hold" the parent's availability when he loses his internal capacity. It's possible to measure the amount of object and self-permanence a three year old has developed. See how long he can function away from the parent without seeing the parent or using the transitional object to evoke the feelings of security and warmth. Most three-year olds can tolerate being away from the dad or mom for one and one half hours up to three hours.

When a child's internal capacity is stretched to this point, he needs actual contact with the nurturing facet of the parent or evocative sensory reminders (transitional objects) of the parent's nurturing presence. Notice how vulnerable the child is, feeling he is "all good" or "all bad."

The building blocks of this internal structure of self are forming from birth to four years of age. This is a critical developmental process. Four-year-olds are just begin to realize that mom or dad can be nurturing, angry, energetic, crabby, and patient. Over time, the child has experienced many different facets of mom. The child can safely function as the separate person that he is—most of the time—because he knows that the parent's protection, security, comfort, and warmth are easily available.

Parents, who are emotionally and/or physically unavailable, can hinder the child's development of a strong, internal sense of self. Then the building blocks of self are absent or weak. The individual, of any age, is vulnerable to difficulty developing and/or sustaining a positive and stable self-concept. That person will also have difficulty sustaining relationships across time, space, changing circumstances, and a range of emotions.

Integration of the Self (object and self constancy) *"There was a little girl who had a little curl right in the middle of her forehead. And when she was good, she was very, very good. And when she was bad, she was horrid."*

This well-known poem describes the self-perception of the average three-year-old. What is implied, but not spelled out is the child's sense that the good Suzy and the horrid Suzy are two separate beings. Before the child has object constancy, she perceives the angry mother as a different, separate being from the nurturing mother. This split perspective represents the child's inability to understand that the angry mom and the nurturing mom are one and the same person. If the child cannot yet perceive the parent as constant, as stable and integrated, she cannot perceive herself as integrated; the good Suzy and the bad Suzy are two separate beings.

Listen to the language of three-year olds caught in the act of stealing a cookie. Suzy tells her mom that her imaginary friend did it. Children of this age **believe** their "fabrications". These children do not yet have parental or self constancy. They have not yet integrated all the facets of themselves. From age three until four or five, children continue to build their object constancy. **What is outside goes inside** and object (or parent) constancy is integrated as self-constancy. It helps to use constancy language, "you are still you, even when you take a cookie. (See the tools section.)

<u>Splitting</u> Normally, children move slowly and surely (with situational setbacks) towards integration of self. **Children who have deficits in their attachments to their primary caregivers cannot develop self-constancy.** These children continue to perceive themselves as incomplete. They continue to split rather than integrate.

If a child perceives herself as valuable, she will split off and deny the bad Suzy until she has self-constancy. If she perceives herself as worthless and does not experience or perceive the parents as valuing her, she will split off and deny the good Suzy. The image that fits the self-perception is experienced as the self. The discordant image is split off. This child will not be able to accept responsibility for her actions until she develops self-constancy. The child develops self-constancy from the capacity of the parent to provide constancy. This growth is slow, spanning several years from toddler age when the object and parent constancy starts forming until the middle elementary years.

Integration is a lifelong journey. All of us have parts we disown or try to disown. All of us have experienced situations that stress our stability and wholeness of self. However, most of us are fortunate enough to be able to maintain our self-constancy or to regroup and pull ourselves together in stressful situations. We experienced the permanence and stability of our parents as we grew up. We developed self-permanence and self-constancy from our experiences with and perceptions of our experiences with our parents.

For neglected or abused children, life is a vicious cycle that can impact generations within a family. When the child experiences the loss or unavailability of the parent, the child's sense of self is based on that instability. Consequently, the child, perhaps now an adult, may have difficulty sustaining a resilient sense of self across a range of experiences or emotions. Split adults cannot experience stable relationships. The split adult perceives others as inconsistent and unavailable. "If you loved me, you would not be angry. If you are angry, you do not love me." This person also experiences self as split, detached, cracked, broken in pieces, crumbled, or crumbling. Whatever aspect of self is evoked in a particular situation is perceived as the whole self; different facets of self are not understood to exist and not available to manage and to adapt to the situation.

This instability of the outer world, as experienced through the relationship with parental figures, is now inside and expressed as a fragile and vulnerable sense of self.

In Adoption: Infants and young children who experience a loss of caregivers are vulnerable to deficits in object-constancy and self-constancy. They experience life as out of their control and cannot accept responsibility for many of their actions. They may be unable to perceive important people in their lives as available to them, even when it is so. A child who has not integrated his sense of self often presents vastly different parts of self to different people. Mom's experience of the child's split may be 80% negative and 20% positive; mom gets the bad Suzy most of the time. Dad's experiences with Suzy are 80% positive and 20% negative. Mom and dad have opposing perceptions of Suzy. They argue about Suzy. Suzy's inability to integrate can cause a split in the marriage. A split child or adult can split a team of professionals.

Two teachers may love Suzy while two other teachers think that Suzy is a disciplinary problem and disruptive to the whole class. They argue about Suzy. When the adults around the split child split, they miss valuable information about the child's dilemma. They miss the opportunity to help the child integrate. The good Suzy and the bad Suzy are different parts of the same child. Both experiences and perceptions of Suzy are Suzy. She needs mom and dad to perceive her as one child with different parts to help her integrate. See the tools section on using parts language.

The child needs assistance developing object constancy and self-constancy (see the section on tools). Split children stress family functioning and can break up the parenting team.

Chapter 8. Clog Dancing (Resiliency) – Developing a Constant Sense of Self Throughout Childhood

Constancy refers to the ability to perceive the parent, and therefore the self, as whole across emotional experiences. A person demonstrates resiliency when he recovers, bounces back, or pulls himself together, using his capacity for self constancy. As the child learns through experience that mom is the same mom whether she is nurturing or angry, so the child learns that he is the same whether successful or unsuccessful, angry or happy, affectionate or withdrawn. The loving part of the parent—no matter the mood—is still available to the child even when there is tension, anger, disagreement, disapproval, and/or physical distance between the parent and the child.

As children grow they reach other usual steps or stages. We've not detailed all of them here because so much of the child's internal self comes from the essential early steps. Also, much of the attachment work depends on being able to see the tiny child in the older child who has missed earlier steps. The chart on the next pages includes additional information on these older ages (6 – 18), read on for more info.

In Adoption Adopted and foster children form their sense of themselves, of their value and worth, based upon their experiences with all primary caregivers, such as birth, foster, and adoptive parents. All adoptive and foster children need to integrate their experiences and perceptions of their birthparents and previous caregivers with their experiences and perceptions of their adoptive parents. Constancy can be tricky to achieve when the previous caregivers were not constant.

The Steps of Attachment and the Impact

Developmental Steps	Typical Developmental Needs	Healthy Parent-Child Interaction	Normal Behavior
The Ballet, Consolidation of Individuation 36 – 54 Months The Clog of Resiliency	The new focus for the child is on building competency. Also initiating contact with others. Her magical and egocentric thinking leads her to feel responsible or to blame herself for whatever happens. The child needs reassurance that he or she is not responsible.	Parents must encourage and support opportunities for children to use their newfound imaginative and creative abilities. They must help the child to separate reality from fantasy, the imagined from the experienced. Consistent, kind, limits. Joined learning of basics, numbers, behavior, etc.	• Regresses to younger behaviors when tired • Vacillates between wanting attention, and rejection of affection • Magical and egocentric thinking • Imaginary "friends" • Can tolerate separations • Infatuated with social life

# of Negligent/Inappropriate Experiences-Chart

Inappropriate/ Negative Experiences Affecting the Child	Resulting Behavior	Best New Parental Response
Parents can get caught in the dilemma of constant correction, to the extent of threatening the child's developing independence. Multiple caregiver changes, moves in foster care or extended family can disrupt the child's sense of constancy and ability to attach. Sometimes a child can "connect" to a difficult parent through the parent's anger or abuse. This neglect or abuse can slow emotional development.	• Chronically oppositional. • Approaches or prefers strangers. • Constantly looking for attention in any way possible – acts spoiled. • Passive and disinterested style of relating-flat affect. • Negative responses to increased contacts outside of the family. • Occasionally regresses-starts wetting again etc. • Struggles between dependency and independence. • Lying – blaming another.	Continue eye-contact games, peek-a-boo and attachment exercises. Use parts language—so the child learns that everyone has many personality aspects: happy, sad, athletic, healthy, smart, tired, short, bored, etc. Parts language helps the child understand that when he acts badly he's not all-bad. (See tools)

The Steps of Attachment and the Impact

Developmental Steps	Typical Developmental Needs	Healthy Parent-Child Interaction	Normal Behavior
6-10 year olds The Square Dance of Belonging and Claiming Continues	Building stability and predicta-bility in primary relationships allowing for expansion of social mastery skills. Support and promotion of indepen-dence while turning to family for equilibrium.	Parents must be "Islands" for the child and support their struggles to learn about self and others. The child must be allowed to caringly face the "up and downs" of new situations and trials. Every child needs a cheerleader. Parents must tolerate and help the child cope with moodiness, strong emotional challenges, and conflicts at this stage.	• Expanded interest in the social world outside of family. • Emphasis on mastery and competency. • Greater controls from within. • Less egocentrism, more realistic thinking.

# of Negligent/Inappropriate Experiences-Chart

Inappropriate/ Negative Experiences Affecting the Child	Resulting Behavior	Best New Parental Response
Maladaptive behaviors can be caused when parents cannot provide a dependable or safe environment. Also, unresolved parental grief and loss issues can affect children Parents who act annoyed or who regard behavior as "on purpose" or see behavior as deliberate and aggressive increase the problem. Losses and abuse can cause child to "get stuck" at earlier steps.	• The child consistently loses things, such as homework (after it's been done), jackets etc. • Extreme changes in mood, attitude, emotional control • Testing the limits, challenging authority, using verbal means to control others • Some day-dreaming, absent-mindedness, and forgetfulness More severe • Disinterest in relationships outside of the family • Overly dependent on "good child" behavior • Lack of knowledge of self, egocentrism, "magical thinking" • Lack of empathy • Premature independence or emotional emancipation • Hard on things, bumps into and breaks things, bumps into people, loses things • Cutting, suicide, running • Bullying behavior • Extreme tantrums	Don't get angry; help the child find things. Don't send her off alone for a time out – it will increase feelings of frustration. Do time outs in sight of you. Go back to the early games of peek-a-boo to learn that things and people continue to exist when out of sight. "Parts" language also works with older kids. Calm response to angry outbursts. Firm, consistent, loving discipline. The child does not understand why he has outbursts and cannot be "reasoned" out of them.

The Steps of Attachment and the Impact

Developmental Steps	Typical Developmental Needs	Healthy Parent-Child Interaction	Normal Behavior
Preadolescent and adolescents Early: 11-14 years Middle 14-16 years Late 16-18 years	Developing autonomy & independence, also, fear of emancipation. Status losses (aware of lacking something others have) are important. Most children struggle with anxiety and confusion over identity. Parents must provide a secure base for transitions to adulthood. Other than infancy, adolescence is the most important time. Your child needs parental support and availability – but it may be harder to give.	As growth occurs "in opposition," parents must be available, supportive, and non-rejecting. Expectations, rules and limits from parents are necessary for the teen to gradually and positively take control of self and behavior. Parents should practice "caring control", set limits in a non-punishing manner, and use a healthy sense of humor in meeting the changing needs of the child.	Early and Middle: • Movement away from family toward allegiances with peers. • Testing, defiance, oppositional and control issues. • Identity and role confusion, "who am I?" Late: • Increased reality testing, but continued risky behavior. • Emotional emancipation • Identity and sexuality are important. • Internal pressure to develop autonomy, competency and self-esteem.

Inappropriate/ Negative Experiences affecting the child	Resulting Behavior	Best New Parental Response
Parents with unresolved issues from their own teen years are at risk for serious problems in parenting their teen. Parents who cope with their teen's near-constant fluctuations and varying demands by being increasingly rigid and inflexible risk a chronic negative relationship with their teen. Contrarily, the too lenient parent is unavailable to set limits or rules to control their teen. Life is unstable. .	• Occasional irritability, unreasonableness, avoidance of consequences • Laziness, self-centeredness • Extreme mood swings • Acute dependency, avoidance of peer relationships, over-reliance on family for identity and self-esteem • Loss, abandonment, and belonging issues • Identity confusion • Sexual interest, and behavior/testing Extreme • Fascination with sex • Depression/ thoughts of suicide • Self abuse/cutting • Drug and alcohol abuse that surpasses the normal experimentation • A drastic drop in grades and school attendance • Runaways, sneaking out, consistent violation of reasonable rules and curfews • Identification with" weird", cultist, overly hostile, or negative groups that interfere with daily functioning	Try to see your child's behavior at its developmental level-for example, 2-year-old tantrums—testing limits. React as you would for the 2-year-old, Redirect if possible. Don't give in to the behavior, allow natural consequences to occur, and when the child turns the behavior around praise and reaffirm your love despite the bad behavior. Rules must be clear, i.e. you need to be home from dates by 12:30 A.M. When rules are violated, sometimes it helps to give your child a selection of consequences. She will feel more in control and be willing to comply. For example, if she's late she might have the choice of grounding for a week or cleaning out the garage. Laugh with your child, play!

Section III. Healing the Adopted Child – The Phases of Attachment in Adoption and a Parent's Best New Responses

<u>Phase One, Great Expectations and Shadow Boxing</u> When the wounded child (two months to adolescence) and the healthy parent(s) first meet, the parent anticipates being effective, helping the child to learn acceptable behaviors and to heal from the pain of the past. Because of prior experience, the child can only anticipate more of what has occurred in the past with previous caregivers. The child enters the interactions with a wounded core—the shadow—full of pain, missing developmental stages, and possessing unhealthy coping skills.

At first you may—or may not—experience a honeymoon period. During this time you'll wonder why anyone worried about attachment issues. However, maladaptive behaviors may show up later. Adoptive parents have described hurt children as often displaying one or the other of two behavior patterns, either: 1. people pleasers or 2. angry most of the time.

People pleasers are much easier to deal with but they too have attachment issues and need your help. Angry children are the ones who try their parent's souls but can clearly benefit from help.

<u>Phase Two, Conflict Begins</u> Many behavior problems that plague the parents of children with "special needs" are normal and expected throughout the early stages of child development. However, persistent negative behaviors at older

ages can disrupt families and distance parents from their children. A child's behaviors can get stuck at an age where she experienced loss or trauma. As a new response, it is very important to view persistent negative behaviors as earlier unmet needs. Parents can identify their child's unmet developmental needs and decide what parenting skills are needed when they understand normal development. The age that the troubling behavior normally occurs is a guideline for developing effective responses. Charting your child's timeline will help you know what to do (see Chapter 9). Also, it's stabilizing to know that no matter where the child is developmentally, she is the same child.

Boundary issues occur when the child's negative/defensive behaviors trigger the parent's reactive/defensive responses. The parent's own self-permanence and self-constancy can be challenged as the parent struggles with intensely negative responses to the child's non-compliance and/or inability to return affection. His sense of self as a "good enough" parent weakens. This is the parent's shadow. The parent may have difficulty recalling that his nurturing side is still present and available.   A parent's self-constancy can weaken in relationships with the non-compliant child.

Any or all of the stages of the parent's self-permanence may also weaken as he struggles with the following issues:
- holding boundaries, (**permeability**);
- coping with multiple roles, (**flexibility**);
- belief that a person can master situations, **(agency)**
- maintaining the capacity to control and contain changing situations (**stability**);
- understanding the difference between the child's emotions and his own internal wounds, (**differentiation**).

58

Phase Three, Meeting the Shadow No adoptive homestudy or child assessment uncovers everything about the potential parents or the child. We all have our hidden parts, our parts that are in shadow even to ourselves. The process of "holding back" and having "hidden parts" is normal and usual. However, a parent's willingness to understand herself will help her cope with adopted children and their developmental needs. A new response to your child would be to talk gently and respectfully about your own parts. Parts language (see tools) helps teach your child to understand his many parts and to deal with them kindly and openly.

If the negative, defensive behaviors between the parents and the child persist too long, parent and child can begin to trigger each other's inner wounds. The wounds of both can become inflamed and grow. The parent can lose her sense of self. Boundaries are violated and permeability is weakened and enmeshment (codependent behavior) and/or disengagement (distancing—inaccessibility) can both occur.

Phase Four, Conquering the Shadow and Healing A more stable parent-child relationship occurs when the parent takes responsibility for his own shadowy responses. As a new response, the parent too must begin to accept and control previously rejected parts of self and heal old wounds. Then his wounded part will grow smaller. Parents don't have to become one with the child (enmesh) to get the child to change. The parent now responds proactively at the first or second sign of boundary pressures, viewing the child's actions as unmet needs and the incident as an opportunity to hold sensory connection and practice new skills.

<u>Phase Five, Parental Self-Care</u> It takes a lot of work to raise a child. We want these tools to be used by all adoptive and foster parents, however, a child with attachment deficits can exhaust even the most experienced person. While you parent, remember the following points, and enjoy the ride.

Positive Responses
- Get enough rest and some private time—you will not be a good parent if you are exhausted. Care for your physical health also—your child cannot afford another loss. Childhood is a marathon, not a sprint.
- Continue positive friendships in your life. This models good relationship-building, teaches self-care and will keep you going during stressful times. No child should have the pressure of being the whole center of a parent's life no matter how needy.
- Don't hide your frustrations; share them with family, friends or your own counselor. Join an adoptive parent support group. Some children have learned to keep "unhealthy secrets." You want your children to be able to talk about feelings and tell if someone hurts them. Model this behavior.
- Don't try to be a perfect parent. Acknowledge your mistakes. This gives your child permission to err and models acceptance of yourself as a person of many parts— not all of which are positive. Remember your child's behavior is not a measure of your ability as a parent.
- Your child will physically grow up no matter how you behave. Accept that you can only do your best. Your parenting cannot always change what has happened in the past nor prevent future hurts. Relax!

- Laugh! Fun and laughter connect you with your child. It also gives you rewards for your efforts. Don't take life—no matter how stressful—so seriously all the time.

Joy then Let-Down   Linda's second adopted child came home two weeks ago. Alyssa was perfect, healthy, responsive, cute, and alert—all the time! Her older son Alan (also perfect in her opinion) comfortably fit into a daily schedule. He took a daily two-hour nap. That naptime belonged to Linda. She used it to relax, catch up on work, and enjoy the quiet.

Unfortunately, little Alyssa seemed unable to settle in at the same time as Alan. On one particularly daunting day with again no respite from the constant demands, Linda found herself sitting on the back porch crying with frustration. She questioned whether she could handle it all. Why wouldn't the kids cooperate? After some serious soul-searching she realized that her mood was the result of the intense effort and emotion of waiting and then traveling to adopt Alyssa, plus the frustration of the child's and her own transition issues. Crying was healthy and normal—and temporary.

Note: If crying persists, be sure to get professional advice. You cannot help your child unless you care for yourself first.

Section IV. New Responses to Old Behaviors, Effective Parenting Tools

Missteps in the dance of attachment can be repaired through the use of effective parenting tools. The following six chapters will help you learn new steps.

Chapter 9. Create Your Child's Timeline to Learn Where to Begin the Dance

Before you read on, create a time-line to help assess your child's needs. This is an activity that uses history to identify possible difficulties with permanency and constancy. Draw the time-line and document your child's age with the corresponding events that took place. Then match each designated age with the normal developmental stage of a child at that age. This activity powerfully represents what did and did not happen in your child's life. The earlier chart of children's developmental needs details the crucial feats for developing and building permanency and constancy. Use it as a model for your child's time line. Remember that the child needs to be able to revisit earlier developmental stages without disapproval. This seemingly "weird" behavior can actually help the child.

Copy the sample chart on the next page. Continue it on throughout the child's life. Add a column where you can identify the stages of learning that need to be revisited or affirmed. Write down your plans and activities.

A Baby Again One recently adopted ten-year-old, Allison, "borrowed" her infant cousin's pacifier and sucked on it when she rode in the car—for a month. This behavior would be normal for a two or three year old dealing with a move or the birth of a new sibling— and it was appropriate for Allison.

Beth's Timeline (Sample)

Age	Normal Need	Adverse Event	Plan of Action
0 to 6 weeks Waltz	Parent available on demand, safety and security	Immediately taken from birth mother.	
2 to 5 months Tango	Parents attached to child, provide stimulation and positive interactions	Attached to foster mom for nine months.	
5 to 9 months Tap Dance	Peek-a-boo and funny faces promote connection and parental permanency. The parent leaves but comes back.	Foster mom was somewhat neglectful. Beth was dirty and had health issues. She stayed in the crib a lot.	
9 - 18 months Two Step	Child ventures out. Parent is different person from self but constant.	Beth went to a new foster mom. She attached to this family.	
18 to 28 months Hip Hop	Child needs certain boundaries. He comes and goes, sometimes exploring and sometime acting as a baby.	This was a good foster home.	
28 to 54 months The Clog	Parents support child's reaching out. Helps him know reality from fantasy.	At 34 months, Beth was placed for adoption with strangers who lived 600 miles away. The transition took only 3 days.	New parents work on connections & permanency with peek-a-boo, funneling and other tools.

Chapter 10. General Adoptive/Foster Parenting Guidelines

<u>**Transition/Bridging**</u>   Parents should explain to the child that his birth parents or former foster parents miss him and were sad when they were not able to continue to parent him. This helps the child find a constant message about himself. The sequence of events in the adopted child's life creates a difficult dichotomy for children to process; birth parents chose not to parent and adoptive parents chose to parent him. Whenever there's a significant change in your child's future, try very hard to help him understand what the change is about, when it will happen, and who will be there for him. Unfortunately, those first transitions—loss of birth parent, orphanage stays, and the adoptive placement—probably had little transition period.

<u>**Culture/Ethnicity/Race**</u>   Learn   about   your   child's country/culture of origin. When your child enters your home she will bring with her practices that may seem strange if you're not aware of them. For example, swaddling is used to soothe babies in many cultures, appropriate hair care is a bonding experience in the African American community, and some Asian and Native American infants have a mark (Mongolian spot) at the bottom of the spine that is usual and not a sign of abuse. You may look, smell, talk and touch differently than earlier caretakers.

<u>**Constancy**</u>   Maintain   constancy,   use   daily patterns, keep promises. Say for example, "I love you and I am angry that you are using the stealing part of you" or "You're using your talking part when I asked you to be quiet." Give non-verbal and verbal indications of your love during conflict or as soon as possible after conflict to give the child sensory evidence   that   your   love   endures   and   is   constant.

Value/Claim   Actively value, enjoy, and delight in your child. Share in random acts of laughter and comfort. Many children with difficult beginnings missed the symbiotic stage of valuing or were never admired just for being. Still others missed the practicing stage of cheering for effort. "No one cheered when I pooped in the potty".

Loss Issues   Teach your children to recognize, label, and safely express their feelings of loss. Recognize the loss of birth parents. Say, "I bet your birth mother thinks of you on every birthday."

Validate   Validate feelings by saying, "I can see that you are sad". You do not have to agree with the feeling to validate the child. Give the child a positive internal label, "You are my good kid, I love you."

Empowerment/Mastery   Build your child's belief in her ability to learn and master skills. Remind your child that she was once not able to do all of the things that she now does well.

Parts of Self   Positively comment on the child's many parts such as their talents, interests, hobbies, moods, mannerisms, traits, and physical features. Talk about your own many parts also.

Support/Expertise   Get help if maladaptive behavior persists, is extreme, or if your child is physically harmful to self or others! Make sure the therapist you use understands adoption/foster care issues. Don't be reluctant to ask the therapist about his or her experience in adoption. If it seems short in time, or if the therapist doesn't seem to think adoption can impact the child, seek out a different professional.

Chapter 11. Enhancing Attachment for Each Stage, the Tempo Accelerates

There are different attachment activities and games that are appropriate for various stages of development. When your child's timeline has helped you understand which stages your child has missed, you can then adapt the activities below to help her revisit—in a safe way—each stage.

Simple games can be adapted for older children if the child's developmental age is younger. Think about ways to adapt the game to fit your child, for example: instead of singing "Farmer in the Dell" together as you might for a two year old, you might take turns making up lines to rap songs with a ten year old. Face each other and try repeating each other's lines, all the lines. Clap hands, and laugh as you do it. The goal is not to get it right, the goal is being together, with joy and laughter.

A. The Slow Waltz (Fog)

Molding Exercises Provide loving touch, smell, comfort, feeding, movement, and sound. This is <u>extremely important</u>. Do finger molds (a brief touch of fingertips with a slight rubbing motion) hand molds, (your hand over her hand softly touching). Finger molds and hand molds help children who are cautious of entering into intimacy experiences. They will often tolerate brief sensory expression of intentional and safe, touch. Side hugs are also sneaky ways to hug the child to your side little by little and encourage touch and full hugs. This type of loving touch is less threatening to children who stiffen up at contact because of physical or sexual abuse.

B. The Tango (Symbiosis)

Positive Interactions Positive interactions give the child the experience of being valued and therefore being valuable without having to perform. The parent's joyous admiration of the toddler's efforts and achievements without judgment, enhances the growing child's self love. Together, positive interactions and joy and admiration for both efforts and accomplishments form the foundation of positive self-image and self-esteem. The child, still perceiving self as one with the parents and yet practicing being different, feels omnipotent. This feeling of power and self-love is normal and healthy, at this stage.

In symbiosis, the essential feature is "the gaze". Gaze into your child's eyes—even if only to catch her eyes for a second. Don't force, don't stare, make eye contact come naturally. Play mirroring games such as patty cake, touching face parts, sing songs, and give nose kisses, (if your child displays opposition to these activities, the parent should go first—always having fun. Interaction should be parent initiated. Give hugs, partial, then full if the child accepts them. You and your child can simply cuddle or just talk, or even watch a movie together—perhaps under a blanket to replicate the warmth and security of the womb.

Funneling Children with attachment problems often seek attention indiscriminately from strangers. When you adopt your child, you might be amazed to see that she is willing to go to anyone in your neighborhood, church or family. You may think, "how wonderful - she is so friendly." But, this behavior usually indicates an attachment problem: the solution is to funnel the child.

Funneling means helping the child revisit the symbiotic stage—learning dependency on only one or two parents. You funnel by not letting the child be held, fed, or comforted by anyone other than you, your spouse, and maybe one sitter, for several months (years sometimes) or until she consistently goes to you to meet her needs.

Ask friends and family to send the child back to you for: food, hugs, permission, sharing, and affection whenever possible. This can be very difficult or uncomfortable to do. Other people don't understand, and in fact think that your child's sociality seems great. Explain the technique. Write plans for funneling: list primary caregivers, identify the child's substitute caregivers. Begin to offer the child (over and over until one sticks) transitional objects to evoke the child's sensory memory of a molding or mirroring connection with the parents. Decide what kinds of affection a substitute caregiver can offer and receive. Think about how the caregiver can evoke the sensory memory of the parents for the child—pictures, toys, etc. The idea is to help the child focus on and learn dependency on the parents. Create a brief ritual for parting whenever it's necessary to leave your child with another.

An Attachment Story Kimberly was adopted as a one-year-old from India. At two, her mom Joan realized that Kim's behavior was different from that of her older children. Kim would ask perfect strangers at the store to "take her to the potty," jumped in the doctor's lap, and never showed stranger anxiety. Although charming to everyone else, Kim's behavior was disturbing to Joan.

One day Joan attended a Holly attachment seminar and stayed afterward. They talked and Holly explained that indiscriminate attention seeking is a sign of attachment deficits. She also explained that attachment could be mended. They started therapy—most of it done at home between parent and child. Joan learned to pick up Kim like an infant and gaze in her eyes while singing. They cuddled, rocked, played—games of all stages—and learned to fall in love. Joan realized that this problem was not her fault. And, she learned how to revisit and heal missed developmental stages. Today Kim is loving and fully attached.

- games are fun ways to pattern the brain for attachment and make up for missed steps.
- Play games that create movement away from and then back to you, for example fetch, tag, squirt gun battles.
- Call out to your child (auditory check in) when she's in another room.
- Go to the child, rub her head and say "HI" (verbal and tactile check in).
- Call the child to come and get a cookie or piece of fruit, (rewarding movement towards the parent figure).
- Help your child check in frequently and refuel—winks, waves, phone calls, etc.
- Set daily check-in routines such as breakfast together, a greeting and discussion after school, or nightly tucking in and story time when going to bed.
- Provide opportunities for the child to relive key stages missed—parent initiated games can help.
- Use parts language to describe feelings, experiences, skills and appearance.
- Connect opposing thoughts, feelings, experiences with "and your angry part is showing and it is not all of you."
- Expect occasional relapses. It's part of this process. Sometimes children can be working on a stage and yet not achieve changes.
- Praise your child's effort, this is essential, not just praise for achievement.
- Understand that your child is beginning to learn to please you when she stops at the boundary (curb) even if she eventually continues.
- Complete multiple repetitions. Older children need both repetitive practicing and continuous praise for their efforts and achievements.

Transitional Objects Begin offering transitional objects that are portable, durable and that evoke a sensory memory of being in contact with the parent. Items such as favorite blankets, teddy bears or pacifiers help the child relive the experience of safety, comfort, warmth, value and joy with the parents. Older children love gifts such as beanie babies, little cars, scarves—all of which are found cheaply at garage sales.

Symbiosis Games (adapted for the child's age)
- Mirroring games; watch and mimic body movements (two rocking chairs across from each other holding hands and singing camp songs).
- Peek-a-boo (even a 10-year-old can be engaged in the rear view mirror of the car by saying, "I love looking at your beautiful brown eyes when you sit in the back seat").
- Fetch it back.
- Roll it back.
- Hide the thimble.
- Play with and master food and utensils (cook and eat together).
- Chase the child, scoop up, sit down and laugh—even a teen likes teasing and wrestling games.
- Cheer for effort.
- Imitate, do all the same things.
- Gentle wrestling.

Building Permanence These activities help the child learn how to hold the memory of a person when out of sight. Play hide the button - briefly hide an object that is not important to the child. Make sure that the "button" reappears in just a few seconds and that you talk or chatter as the button is out of sight, creating the sensory overlap of the Fog Stage of attachment that is so critical as the foundation for permanence. Try three, five, or seven repetitions (or more) at a time. Be sure to be playful and to try to modulate your voice and your expression up and down, soft and louder showing curiosity, joy and delight. These activities foster representational permanence and help the child with constancy.

C. The Tap Dance (Differentiation) 5 to 9 Months

The baby at eight or nine months is more awake and alert and begins to differentiate between family and strangers. She looks out from the lap or explores as she creeps around on the floor. Your child, adopted at an older age may be differentiating at a later age but still needs the same steps.

The child is learning that the parent's safety, comfort, warmth, value, and joy continue to exist. Play "hide the parent" to help build parent permanence. Pay attention to the child's defensive reactions. Hide a part of you (e.g. head, feet, hands) under a blanket or all of you for a few seconds. Help the child find you with modulation of vocal tone and expression. Rapid discovery can be alternated with blanket work: parent and child stay under the blanket together creating a symbiotic experience of mirrored intimacy. Some children love to be able to tell the parent where to hide, "Daddy hide behind the sofa." Then they know exactly where to find you—wow. Play peek-a-boo quickly with delight and surprise when you uncover your face. Try to uncover your eyes in two to four seconds, again three to five to seven repetitions.

D. The Two Step (Practicing) 9 to 18 Months

Play hide and seek the normal toddler way. For example, when the child hides he makes noise and is partially or completely visible and the parents talk as they search and quickly find the child. This builds self-permanence. Parents "hide" in the same way: with sound and some visibility. Child may peek when parents are hiding. Remember your child needs to peek until their permanence is stronger.

Checking In

Children with attachment issues may not automatically go through the toddler check-in stage. Initiate a check-in plan: method, frequency, child's part, and fun behavior. For example: with a three year old wave and wink often. Your child should wink back—then give a hug or a treat. Do this until the child learns to check in with you. Checking in teaches differentiation and is profoundly rewarding for the parent's sense of attachment.

Transitioning Games

- Freeze tag. The "it" person tags the child, he freezes until another player tags him to let him go. It's a chance to go away and come with a sense of belonging and fun. It also helps to practice changing body state from hyper to calm.
- "Mother/Father May I" and "Simon Says," teach interaction with parents, helps with listening skills, setting boundaries and following parent's directions.
- Red Rover, Red Rover. Two teams (can be two people each) line up across from each other, hold hands and say "Red Rover come over." One person from the opposing team runs across and tries to break through the line.

Activities to Build Boundaries

1) Describe how harsh physical boundary violations can be, e.g. the stove is hot, it hurts to touch it.
2) Play creeping games. Imitate a tortoise, a soft gentle bunny, a tired puppy.
3) Play Head and Shoulders, Knees and Toes.
4) Teach emotional boundaries and empathy as you watch a movie, read a book, or observe people in person. Ask, whose feelings are these? How does the character in the movie feel? Why didn't she say no?

Practice

- These activities and games must be repeated over and over just like you do with an infant.
- Rejoice in your child's efforts. Cheer for any tiny attempt at a skill.
- Celebrate effort, not just success.
- Building with Lego's and/or blocks creates numerous chances for effort, frustration, failure and success.
- Floor play—cars, Star Wars, Legos—where you play with the child is important. Floor play puts you at the child's level and promotes symbiosis.
- Give your child words, expressions and movements for failure and frustration. Expressions like: "What a bummer!" "Uh, oh, spaghetti O's" are very appropriate. Even slapping the floor is adequate for expressing negative emotions and handling frustration.

E. The Hip Hop (Rapprochement) 18 to 36 Months

The most important treatment technique for **rapprochement** is to build parent and child constancy. Whether you're dealing with rapprochement in a toddler or in an older child, always react to any inappropriate behavior as you would to a child of that developmental age. For example, a ten-year-old acting like a four-year-old should be treated like a four-year-old, redirected, with short logical consequences, and given a reassuring hug.

Parents need a **great deal of support and encouragement** during rapprochement. Friends can help by listening to you complain and yet knowing that the next day you will be all right.

Behaviors that your child had once stopped may return, not as a deliberate act, but as a subconscious test of the attachment. It is important to understand how the raging, wetting, lying, stealing, etc. is different than it was before. For example, raging in rapprochement usually happens less often and resolves faster than raging before this stage. These seemingly insignificant differences are very important. They represent that your child has attached and she now needs to test this attachment.

Belonging and claiming goes on throughout all of childhood and rapprochement can occur at any age. Part of a parent's job is to be your child's cheerleader. Some children in their early years never had someone who "cheered when they pooped in the potty." Cheer now no matter what step your child is currently processing.

Shadowing and Darting – Older Child Version Maria was 11 and suffered from early deprivation and abuse. One-day mom told her to go to bed as usual. Maria said "no" and ran to the living room. After a calm reminder, she still refused. Knowing that sometimes oppositional behavior really signals a need to connect and trying to remember how she would deal with a three-year-old, her mom started to tease her good naturedly. She threatened to carry Maria to bed—even though Maria weighed more than mom. This is a little joke between them. When Maria said no again but with a laugh in her voice, mom went and pulled her by the legs off the chair on to a pillow and across the room to the stairs—laughing all the while. (Don't do this if child isn't signaling play—but playful touch is often therapeutic).

When they got to the stairs, mom stopped and told Maria again to go to bed. Maria begged to be pulled down the stairs. Mom refused. Maria wrapped herself around mom's legs and refused to let go. What a sight, a 5 foot, 7 inch, 140 pound girl hanging onto mom's legs. Remembering how small kids always want to ride on parent's legs, her mom touched and tickled Maria until with laughter she let go. The whole connection process took about 15 minutes but turned a potential confrontation into fun.

Rapprochement Games

- Chase, capture and release.
- Shadowing and darting games. Tag with hiding and jumping out—then turning and running.
- Square dance (or any other dance) come close, move away, spin and come close again.

Parts Language This is a technique of specifying one aspect or part of your child rather than referring to her as a whole. For example, instead of saying, "It was fun playing tag." You would say, "I had fun seeing you use your playing and athletic parts." Your child's behavior will improve when you consistently use parts language!

An individual is made up of many parts, i.e. happy, sad, creative, old, blond, angry, musical and more. Well-adjusted people learn that one type of behavior or feeling does not define the whole person. Children who have constancy problems believe themselves to be <u>all</u> mad and worthless when acting mad. They also believe that the parent is all mad when acting mad. Use of parts language helps the child understand that even when the angry part is present she still has many other positive parts—and so does mom. She will not feel so hopeless and worthless when she is able to remember her other parts. She will turn her anger around more quickly.

1) Use parts language to promote constancy.
2) Use parts language to refer to many of your child's different parts: silly parts, great parts, not so great parts. Say: "I like the jokey part of you; You're using your problem solving part; That must be your sad part; I feel angry with that mean part of you."

3) Balance each negative such as, "I don't like..." with a positive "I do like...".
4) Use parts language when you talk about everybody, not just about your child.
5) Avoid only using parts language to refer to just unacceptable parts.
6) Stay connected, with sensory connections, touches, even when angry, tired, etc.
7) Even brief sensory connections—a wink, pat—are fine.

Parts activities

- List all of your parts and the child's - be creative - i.e. wiggly part.
- Trace the body or take a picture and draw and /or write in parts.
- Use analogies and metaphors of the parts of a whole, (e.g. the dog's parts, the cat's parts, parts of an ocean, parts of a house).
- Cut geodes (stones with crystals inside) as a "whole" and discover parts you like and parts you do not like inside.
- Create an origami cootie catcher or modern art self-sculpture that can open and close and examine the parts inside.
- Say, "hank you for using your listening part," or "You are using your listening part. I really appreciate it."

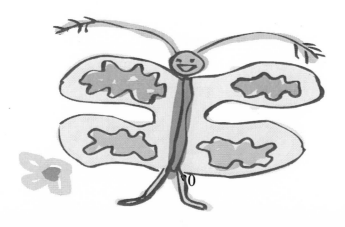

A Girl of Many Parts Susie had very poor self-esteem. At age 12, she had been through abuse, abandonment and multiple caregivers. Her parents used the parts language to help her understand that when she was angry or acted badly she wasn't <u>all bad.</u>

One day she came home from school and informed her parents that she needed a costume for a class play. Her mom asked her to describe the costume or draw a picture. Susie couldn't. She insisted that they go directly to the fabric store and she would then be able to explain. At the store she started pulling bolts of fabric off the shelves, at last picking 18 different ones. Her mom was befuddled until Susie said, "the blue is my sad part, the baby pink is my baby part, the tiger stripe is my angry part, the pink sheer is my feminine part, the dog print is my animal loving part, the Native American is my native part, and the yellow happy face print is my happy part. I want this dress to show all my parts because the play is about feelings."

Susie's mom happily constructed a dress "of many colors" for her to use at school. In the play, Susie explained to the other children that, "people are made up of many parts, not all good or all bad but rather many shades and patterns of color." Her parents rejoiced, Susie really understood. The simple use of language had made an impression.

<u>Joined Learning</u> Joined learning is the spontaneous, encouraging, playful and nurturing way we teach toddlers facts, skills and feeling states. Joined learning is doing the task for the child, while encouraging the child to join in. Joined learning is helping the child find the answer, with encouragement and joy.

The Problem: Certain children experience extreme anxiety when answering questions. These are often the kids who have not developed object or parent constancy. Multiple placements result in uncertainty about how important people will react when questions are asked—because the child feels little constancy. Joined Learning is a tool that can be used to address this problem. Here's an example:

Sam came to his foster parents home 12 months earlier at age 5. He could not count, write his name and did not know the alphabet. When Sam started school his parents were confident, after working with him individually, that he could manage school at grade level. The second month of school Sam read a beginning reader out loud to his reading group and then to the whole class. Two months later Sam's teacher asked him to read the same book for a class demonstration. Sam stood in front of class: he fidgeted, shuffled his feet, and pulled at his trousers, but he did not read. Sam's teacher prompted him with the first word. He said he did not know the words. Sam's teacher reminded him that he had read that same book many times. "Sam, you do know the words." She whispered. The Headmaster suggested that Sam was nervous to read in front of him. Sam shook his head and insisted he did not know the words. Sam stood there with a blank look on his face. Everyone decided that Sam had stage fright. It was an awful experience.

The next week Sam got almost all the words wrong on his spelling test. Following that, he missed simple words in reading class. Sam was frequently failing or not responding to questions and words that his parents and his teacher 'knew he knew'. Everyone decided that Sam was being oppositional. The more his teacher and parents prodded him the more he "refused to answer".

Sam was not being oppositional; he was not simply refusing to answer. Sam was experiencing a temporary inability to recall what he knew when questioned by people he cared about. None of this is conscious. The child's limbic brain shuts down the passageways to the stored concrete knowledge. In that moment, in that situation, with that important person, the child cannot access the stored memory where the knowledge is held.

A child without constancy cannot help this reaction and further prodding makes it worse. The child freezes or becomes rigid and oppositional. The child feels shamed and abandoned. The solution is for the parent to retreat to joined learning techniques.

Toddlers and preschoolers learn many of their early lessons through joined learning. Think about how we teach colors. "This school bus is yellow. It is a yellow school bus." After many repetitions we ask: "What color is the yellow school bus?" Or we might say "What color is the school bus? Pause for a second, "The school bus is yellow!"

We repeat this process over and over in many different ways, gradually getting to the point where we pause longer after asking the question than we did in the early stages of teaching. If the child gets stuck or if the child answers incorrectly we gently provide the correct answer, often having the child repeat it with us. At first children guess, or look at us for hints, which we give freely. Gradually, we observe the growth of the child's knowledge; confidence in his knowledge; and a sense that even if he does not answer or if he gets it wrong, we, the important teaching adults, will still value him. Joined learning helps build constancy.

In a new situation, a child who missed joined learning in the past feels as if the adults in her life now will disconnect, disappear or withhold the relationship if she gets the problem wrong, so she freezes. When this reaction appears, the new relationship must be reinforced through joined learning techniques. New teachers or new parents should revert to joined learning techniques to help the child get over this really frustrating problem. A focus on the problem without using these safer, less threatening techniques can reinforce the child's highly frustrating and dysfunctional reaction.

Chapter 12. Validation – Becoming Your Child's Cheerleader

Validation is a component of the ongoing step of belonging and claiming. It's extremely important and it must continue throughout childhood. It signals to your child that you are actively listening and that you are working hard to accurately receive the important feeling messages that she is sending. Validation also signals acceptance and enhances communication and intimacy. It conveys the message that:

> *" I see you feel bad, I don't understand why, but I love you and will be here if you need me."*

> *"I don't see things the way you do. I would probably act differently if this happened to me. It makes me feel uncomfortable to see you so angry (sad, lonely, etc.)."*

> *"I understand those are your emotions, not mine."*

Your task as a listener is to hear, recognize, accept, and reflect your child's emotions. Focus on her. You may offer your personal perspective as your own view or experience, but stay focused on the child. Parts language can also be used when practicing validation. For example, "you are using your angry part and it's okay to be angry, It's not okay to use your hitting part. Do you think you can you find your calm part?"

Understand and tell your child that all feelings are valid and you accept them, but also explain that some responses may be unacceptable.

What if you don't understand the feelings? To validate your child's feelings, you don't have to understand the feelings. Validation is simply recognizing and accepting feelings. If you withhold validation, you essentially make the relationship about yourself and the hidden message you send says that her feelings are not valid unless they match yours.

What if you disagree with the feelings? It's usually easier to validate people whose reactions are similar to your own. When you disagree with your child's feelings you may reject her feelings by denial. When you disagree, you may judge her emotions as too much, too little, or inappropriate. Rejection of your child's feelings is most often experienced as rejection of her whole being.

What happens when you judge your child's feelings? When you make the judgment that her emotions are wrong because you disagree with her reactions, you stop listening to her and begin to pursue your own agenda. When you make the judgment that she shouldn't feel a certain way, you imply that the other person's emotional perceptions are flawed. This can teach the child to distrust her own perceptions. It is important to consider another view. Stating your perceptions too early in the exchange decreases the process of considering alternatives.

What if you're uncomfortable with your child's feelings?
Managing your own emotional reactions to your child's feelings can be complex. It can be particularly difficult to validate her feelings when you feel uncomfortable with the emotions

86

being expressed. You may feel particularly uncomfortable if the feelings being expressed trigger emotions that you are unable or unwilling to experience. You may feel powerless and you don't know how to help your child.

Don't over-react. Practice validation. Remember your own emotional reaction and work on it at a later time with a trusted friend or therapist.

Validation Steps

✓ Listen to the words, (verbal communication.)
✓ Pay attention to the tone, pitch, volume, and excitement of the voice, (non-verbal communication.)
✓ Observe body language, look at the posture, movement, and tension of the child's face, limbs, and the trunk of the body, for example a child who leans away or obsessively taps the floor.
✓ If the emotions being communicated to you (both verbally and non-verbally) match, you have recognition.
✓ Reflect back, express your recognition and acceptance to the other person as soon as possible. "I see that you are mad, sad, glad...I hear that you are very nervous...You sound like you are really excited"... Reflection demonstrates to the other person that you are listening and that her feelings have been acknowledged.
✓ Accept the feelings being expressed as the other person's feelings, not your own. You may share similar feelings or you may have opposing feelings. Say, "It's okay to be angry but it is not okay to hit."
✓ When verbal and non-verbal messages do not match, express recognition of all of the emotions you have identified such as when the other person says they are angry but they are smiling. Say that you are receiving mixed messages to show that you are listening and allow the other person to hear how he is being perceived.

Practice Like every other skill you choose to develop, validating the people in your life takes practice. Scripting is a useful tool. Choose a situation where you feel that you missed the mark or overreacted to another's feelings. Imagine what you could have said if you had time to draw your response from the healthiest part of yourself. Write down one or more phrases that accomplish your goal on a 5x7 index card. Practice your script often and keep those healthy, validating responses in accessible locations near you where you might have an exchange of feelings. Gradually, you will learn how to spontaneously validate the other person's feelings some of the time. When you are unable to do so, you can always go back to the child later and say what you wish you would have said.

Chapter 13. Discipline Strategies – What's Outside Goes Inside

The purpose of discipline is to learn to control ones self in different environments and in different circumstances. Parents need to separate concepts of CONTROL and DISCIPLINE. Control battles are parental issues because society expects parents to control their children. Discipline means teaching, not punishing or coercing. It also needs to be consistent. What you do about any single incident is not as important as what you teach on each occasion. Punishment may need to be part of discipline and it should promptly follow the misbehavior, be short, and respect the child's feelings. Always reconnect in a positive way with your child soon after the conflict.

Sometimes there is a need to stop a frightening behavior. However, don't think that stopping the behavior is all that is needed. Visit an episode or behavior in a broad and facilitative way, not scolding or lecturing but instead asking what can be learned. Think about what parts of yourself you forgot, what would help you remember? Practice these new behaviors.

Assess Your Child's Level of Self-Discipline It's helpful to review the levels of discipline that the child has already reached. Remember, very early lack of boundaries – normal for a two-year-old – may also show up in your ten-year-old. Remembering your child's developmental level will help you react appropriately to an older child. Decide whether:

1. Your child does not know there is a boundary at all, therefore crosses it, and has to be brought back.
2. Your child now knows there is a boundary but teases and smiles while breaking the rule. The message is

89

that the child needs you to stop her without anger. She recognizes that there is a rule, but can't stop breaking it.

- It may look like defiance, but it is not.
- She is displaying a need.
- She knows there is a boundary, says "no" and looks at you. (These behaviors show that the child needs help in keeping the boundary and the child has a real sense of inner turmoil.)
- Practice the skill that is weak. For example, stopping and giving a "high five" just before shopping to strengthen a child's resistance to her shoplifting part.

3. Your child recognizes the boundary, says "no" and moves away. (She has begun the capacity not only to know that a rule exists, but to also follow the rule.)

Communicating clear boundaries takes away uncertainty. If adults are ambivalent—enforcing rules erratically because they are tired, or unsure, the child recognizes indecision and won't learn clear boundaries as quickly.

Understanding Discipline and the Emotionally Injured Child

A   The development of self-discipline gives us the capacity to shape and manage our own behavior and make good choices about our behavior.

B.   Adoptive parents generally learned discipline from modeling in their families of origin.
- Adopted children entering a new family system often come from family systems and/or institutions with dramatically different standards of acceptable

behavior and rules of discipline and punishment. Some have no standards at all.

- Adopted children may have delays in mastery over impulse behaviors and frustration tolerance due in part to instability in their sense of self-permanence.

C. Ineffective or vacillating discipline tends to reinforce unacceptable behavior.

- A child who needs attention will get it even if it is with negative behavior. Negative behavior gains increased attention and intensity of emotion.
- Children, even insecure children, need limits. Parents need to be calm, consistent, and effective when setting limits.

D. Discipline, especially punishment with disapproval and/or anger, can temporarily decrease object (parent) constancy—and the child's basic security.

- Even after being with their new family for quite a while, adopted children often have reduced or weak constancy (belief that parents will love them no matter what happened). After correction reconnect quickly with your child's loving part.
- It's important to set limits, choosing which behaviors most need to be managed—not sweating the small stuff. Be concerned about a child that throws toys at another person rather than worrying when a child doesn't put away the toys. Save serious discipline for really important transgressions (i.e. pick your battles).
- Do not ask the child "Why did you throw the toy?" as the child cannot tell you. Instead, give possible explanations to the child such as; "I think you did this because...", "I did this because..." Tell the child, "I will

help you stop kicking the wall," instead of telling the child to stop the behavior on their own.

- Remind the child that he has many parts and only one part misbehaved. "That must have been your really angry part that made you kick the wall. You can use your words when you are angry and then I'll understand better. Thank you for listening, your listening part is really working well."

These techniques enhance constancy and limit blame, shame and conflict. Remember you are planting seeds of thought and it may take hundreds of repetitions to learn.

❏ Be patient and consistent with your child's experience of love (object constancy) but still enforce the rules.

❏ Demonstrate acceptance. However, be careful. Acceptance doesn't mean lack of discipline, rather it means setting clear standards, enforcing them repeatedly and gently but also continuing to love and accept the child despite bad behaviors.

❏ Make consequences logical.

❏ Make consequences funny, surprising, and novel.

❏ Remember any interruption in a child's activity is a "time out."

❏ Model good self-care and self-discipline. Practice your own stress reducing techniques.

❏ Make sure that the adult relationships in the child's life are healthy.

❏ As much as possible, interact positively, share joy, and express values both verbally and non-verbally. This strengthens attachment.

- Give greater intensity to positive behavior rather than to negative behavior. Make sure you provide five to seven positive exchanges for each negative exchange.

- Avoid rescuing the child if they aren't in danger. Give emotionally age appropriate help to solve the problem.

- Children will not change first; you must modify discipline tactics in order for children to modify their behavior.

- Don't expect changes anytime soon—have a wait and see attitude—remember how long it took for the child to learn inappropriate behaviors.

- Anxiety (e.g. being sent away for a time out), and/or loss of a parent figure (grief) can set up barriers to learning.

- Remind yourself about the child's developmental level. It's much easier to be patient if you understand that your 10-year-old is really behaving at a 4-year-old level. For example, after a 4-year-old has a tantrum, she probably wants you to hug and reassure her. Do that after the dispute has been resolved with the 10-year-old.

- Discipline needs to be appropriate for <u>both</u> the child's developmental stage and chronological age.

- Consider ways to evaluate the need that the child is demonstrating through the unacceptable behavior. If possible, ask the child what is needed.

- Give children choices whenever possible—it helps them feel powerful and teaches good decision making skills.

- A traditional "time out in his bedroom" for an unattached child seems to confirm that you too will send him away. Keep him in the same room and send him to a time out chair where he can see you (generally one minute for each year of age).

- Plan and practice discipline strategies ahead of time.

- Scripting can help you change your behaviors from reactive to proactive and help carry out pre-planned techniques. Write brief instructions to yourself on index cards to be used when the child exhibits behavior that pushes your buttons.

- Express yourselves through "I messages." "You did," sounds blaming and shaming. Saying "I feel angry because the dirty dishes are still in the sink...", "I am going to...", "I hope that you make better choices next time: I know you can..." keeps the focus off the child and on the behavior and its effect.

- Discipline should shape the behavior - not simply punish. Practice correct behavior immediately – "do overs."

- Any consequence needs to be within the bounds of what can be held without resentment by the child—corporal punishment is not okay. A seriously abused child can react with rage and feel terror if spanked, hit, or grabbed.

- Uncontrolled, reactive angry responses from the parent can be very scary. It changes the child's experience of the natural consequences and changes the dynamics of the lesson. It teaches uncontrolled anger.

- If you or the older child/teen has trouble talking about transgressions without blowing up, go to a café for ice cream and talk there. Holding a discussion in public (but out of earshot of the other customers) tends to keep everyone more reasonable.

- Reaffirm love soon or immediately after each disciplinary action or anger exchange.

- Keep the pathway between unacceptable behavior and the consequences free from anger and irritation as much as possible.

- A child with no sense of permanency will have extreme difficulty with transitions. Anticipate increased problem behavior in chaotic situations. Make gradual transitions whenever possible. Always discuss changes ahead of time.

- 1, 2, 3 Magic. Counting 1, 2, and 3 and then putting a toy away helps to calm and manage the child's behavior through distraction. This is used at nursery age. "I am going to count 1-2-3…..(this is done calmly even if you're not feeling calm, but counting slowly helps!) Now I'm going to put the toy away." The object is to calm and manage behavior. This technique is a way to practice and teach safe transitions.

- One minute scolding. Take approximately 30 seconds to express displeasure. Start with saying, "I feel frustrated… because you chose to or chose not to…". Repeat three or four times, then change tone and body language for 30-second positive message. "I really enjoyed reading together yesterday", or "I appreciate that you called home when you were going to be late."

- Do the unexpected when a child exhibits unacceptable behavior. For example, if the child screeches, screech louder—no words and not directly at the child (not for a child over seven). If a child makes a face, play the face back to the child with humor. This must be done in a way which respects the child rather than mocking him.

- As children learn acceptable behavior, they need to feel a sense of mastery and achievement – be a cheerleader.

- Use humor to defuse tense situations.

- If the child is difficult to reason with, write a note. Make it a brief factual note but ended with a positive message, Love, Mom/Dad.

- Use "do-overs:" When the child crosses a boundary, ask him to do it again. "You forgot to say please, try a do over." This places the emphasis on practicing the skill or behavior and helps the child to have feelings of competency and success.

Internalization   Internalization means bringing parental boundaries and enforcement into the child's mind.   When boundaries are internalized, the child feels safe because then she trusts that she can protect herself.   You know you've succeeded when the child internalizes limits. Your long-term attitudes and expectations are key in the internalization process.   Predictive Success—stating, "you will learn" or "you will manage this" is positive.   Stating, "three strikes and you're out" is not positive.

Predictive success is about delivering expectations with a calm attitude.   Remaining firm and telling the child that you will help her out until she can control it herself.   It is a crucial element of helping children establish their inner control.   The message becomes "you can do it in the future."

- All children internalize what they are told and what they experience—what's outside goes inside.
- Parents should try to understand the child's experience in the previous situation, figure out the adaptive behavior the child developed.   Behavior that helped before may now be maladaptive.   For example, sexual abuse victims often wet the bed.   Even though it's done unconsciously, it works to keep people away and smells familiar (secure).
- You, as the adoptive parent/caregiver, must help build the child's ego on your own good, solid internal image. If you have unresolved issues, get help to develop your own insight.
- Some children are afraid to listen.   Was your child able to receive what was offered? If not, try making your comments (positive or negative) more concrete and specific.   "You put all your toys away, hurrah." rather than "You did a good job."   Play peek-a-boo to establish

safety. Use parts language to remind your child of your ongoing loving connection to all her parts.

Progress, One Step at a Time   Lisa age 13 has lived in her new home now for three years. After the honeymoon period where she was extremely repressed, she started to do bizarre things to express feelings and attract attention. Her parents worked hard at remaining positive, constant, consistent, while guiding her—like a three or four year old—into appropriate behaviors.   She had no boundaries about property and stole small items. Bob and Sue used consistent consequences when she took things but also took her shopping at the dollar store to buy trinkets—many of which reminded Lisa of important loved ones. She no longer steals.

Lisa used to act up at family events, so Bob and Sue would take her out of the situation or ignore her behavior (just like a two-year-old) until she acted appropriately. They looked for every possible good thing to give her a compliment about and encouraged other family members to do this also. She seldom exhibits attention-seeking behavior now and interacts with the family group much better than before. She is really a part of the family.

For three years now, when Lisa threw a tantrum, her parents calmed her down, talked about her angry part, encouraged her to try and understand what feelings had provoked the behavior, and rewarded quick turnarounds. It helped them to

99

think about her behaviors as that of a two to four year old. She still has angry episodes but they are shorter, less intense, non-violent, and she turns her behaviors around faster. They talk about her progressing from a two-year-old to now six-year-old behaviors.

Last week Lisa bought a card for her parents. It had a picture of a Dalmatian on the front. Inside it said "See all my spots, I love you that much!" Along with the card Lisa said, "Keep this and when I'm being bad, read it so you remember how much I love you." That's progress and attachment.

Chapter 14. Responses to Specific Behavior Problems – Getting Tired

Ignoring Parents If your child is 10 to 13 years of age but looks through you or ignores you, he is revisiting the six to 18 month task of building permanence.

What to Do:

- Take into account the survival strategies (fight, flight or freeze) that a child may have developed when working on permanence.
- Stay connected, even if just maintaining a presence in the room. Catch his eye, whenever possible, wink or say "I love you," or deliver a compliment, "your hair is cool."
- Maintain interaction at a level that does not cause fight, flight, or freeze.
- Use a moderate voice and gentle physical presentation.
- Don't send the child off alone as punishment. Using a time out chair in the room with the parent works best.
- Remember, if the child doesn't have permanency, the parent doesn't exist when out of sight and this is extremely fear provoking.
- Punishment alone doesn't help internalize learning. The child is incapable of "going to his room to think about what he has done".
- Don't respond to your child's behaviors with frustration and anger, it cuts away the child's experience of the constancy of his parent's love.
- Use parts language.

Stealing This behavior reflects the lack of permanence and the consolidation of individuation step—your child is taking a part of you, a person they deem to be important as he moves away from you. See the glossary for a definition. The object is taken to hold the sense/the memory of you the parent or another person. Your child – no matter the chronological age – may still be doing earlier developmental work. If your child is stealing absolutely anything, then the developmental stage is under 10 months. Remember how you child proofed your home at this age because the child gets into and takes whatever they want. Childproof it again putting valuables/keys/personal treasures in locked places. One parent lost her too-small engagement ring when her newly adopted 8-year-old took it to play in the yard. She still resents the loss.

To help a child at an older age your approach must be gentle and firm just like you would treat a 10-month-old. Assess the quality and purpose of the stealing:
- What is she taking (money, food, or weapons—do we need to worry about safety)?
- Who is she taking from (parents, school, or anybody)?
- What does she do with the objects that she takes (sells items to get income for drugs or more common, hide them or give them away to "friends"...like a toddler)?
- Does she take food to save it to eat at night?

Typical ten month to three year old development
- At this stage a child would be doing permanency work and the child has no sense of property.
- It is quite likely that older children who steal never used transitional objects at the proper stage.
- When these children lose an object, they simply take another.

- When these children lose something by hiding it to keep it safe, it is out of sight and existence so they have to take again.

What to Do:
Remember that with young children taking happens over and over again—time and repetitions are not shorter or less often with older children.
- Childproof the house.
- Set clear boundaries and use parts language.
- Give children transitional objects such as cheap things that can be replaced—but the object should have been worn, used, and perceived as yours.
- Teach boundaries by taking back precious objects and helping children return things.
- Stay connected; help the child as you would a 2-3 year old. Don't nag, use a little humor and be clear about what you see.
- Impose short consequences.
- Don't ask, "did you steal?" if you know the answer, the child will be trapped into lying. Act on what you believe is true.

Lying Lying, even when caught in the act, is one of the most common and persistent behaviors of children who have experienced some trauma, neglect, or loss. This type of lying is normal at age's three to five. At that age children should be gently, firmly, and repeatedly taught to tell the truth. Many of the lies told by older children represent one or more of the missed developmental tasks of three to five-year- olds. These developmental tasks are: learning the ability to tell fantasy

103

from reality in the face of strong emotions, understanding that a person does not cause all of the events in his world, and gaining the ability to develop object constancy. (Object or parental constancy is the experiential faith that the caregiver's love, warmth, comfort, and security is still available even when the child's behavior angers the caregiver: in parts language, "mommy's loving part still exists even when I am using my angry part," or, "I am angry and I love you!")

Our reactions to children who lie are influenced by our belief that older children should not lie. If a parent understands the needs that the behavior expresses, this helps to mitigate our adverse reactions to the behavior. This is not to say that once you identify your child's missed stages and unmet needs, you will never again experience frustration and impatience with the lying. Be patient, this technique takes time and practice. By using troubled behaviors to form an educated hypothesis about the child's needs, you will be able to become much more proactive as you respond to your child's lying behaviors. Map out your intervention goals and return to those goals often.

What to Do:
- When caught in the act, don't ask the child if he lied;
- Be firm, tell your child that lying is not acceptable.
- Use gentle humor.
- Use short consequences.
- Maintain connectedness through hug or touch.
- Don't lie to the child. Practice openness and honesty.

Violence/Self-Harm/Fire-Starting

Remember, most adopted children never exhibit these extreme behaviors but early deprivation can occasionally cause scary times.

What to do These are behaviors that are so extreme that a parent facing any of these actions or threats of action should get professional help for the child. Although it might not seem so serious with a four to six year old—and he may be easier to contain—depression or violence still warrants professional help. If a threat of suicide or violence is made—particularly by an older child—err on the side of caution and contact emergency services 911 or a hospital emergency room.

When seeking professional help, ask for a therapist who has experience with adoption issues. Make sure that he or she understands missed developmental steps and has experience helping adopted and foster children. Therapists without special training in these areas may be quick to label a child and simply provide pills. Medications might be part of a treatment plan but it's also necessary to work through missed developmental steps. Generally speaking, simple talk therapy, or medication alone, without revisiting missed steps, doesn't work well with a child who is having problems with constancy and permanence.

Section V. Responses to Specific Behaviors

Troubling Behavior	Step/Age Where Behavior is Usual	Age Where Behavior is Problematic	Child's Unmet Need
Averts Eyes	Briefly in fog and occasionally in rapprochement.	Anytime.	Permanence, and trust.
Rigid Body When Held	Occasionally during fog and rapprochement when feeling angry.	Infant to adult.	Permanence, Fog: has not yet internalized safety, comfort and warmth. Constancy: "I lose myself if I hug you because my anger is all of me in this moment."
Clinging	Symbiosis: brief cling approaching new situations.	Toddler and up.	Permanence, fears loss of parent, cannot feel parent's existence when out of sensory contact.
Lap Hopping, Indiscriminate Affection	Fog, very early symbiosis.	Past infancy.	Permanence, Does not yet understand that safety, comfort and warmth all come through the parents.
Chameleon, different faces, people pleaser	Symbiosis, chameleon behavior suggest premature differentiation (moving out of symbiosis early due to change in or unavailability of caregiver).	Past toddler age	Representational object permanence
Lying	3 to 6 years. Learning reality is different from fantasy.	Consistently during 3 to 6 years or frequently at older ages.	Constancy; no parent constancy, child fears loss of nurturing parent, no self constancy: child's effort to deny negative self, thinks that when bad she's all bad.

Parent's Usual Response and Feelings	Parent's New Response	Treatment Interventions
Feels rejected; inadequate as parent.	Understands, remains constant and loving—doesn't take it personally.	Peek-a-boo; blanket hide and seek and blanket cocoon; catch child's eyes and make positive comments.
Feels rejected and angry.	Understands, doesn't force touch but keeps it brief and loving.	Massage, beginning with brief touch on small area of the body; unforced. Briefly stroke resistant body part; sideways hug.
Rejection, pushing away. Parents may unconsciously reinforce clinging behavior.	Parent explains that mom will come back later.	Bird's nest game, mama bird goes away and she comes back and you are still you.
Rejection, jealousy, fearful for child's safety. Sometimes parents may think the child is wonderfully friendly.	Funnel child to the parent—the parent fills all child's needs so she knows source of comfort and forms a bond.	Funneling and symbiotic games: peek eye; dance; hands together and apart; mother may I?
Frustration and safety concerns; often does not feel in love with child; feels as if no real person is inside the child; annoyance.	Understands the child is not manipulating on purpose, rather is trying to develop a sense of self	Use parts language and symbiotic games; "the part of you that__;" nose kisses. The child often needs a lot of fog and symbiotic holding, firm daily structure.
Feels it's a deliberate offence; the child has no morals.	Sees the behavior as a reversion to earlier years and treats behavior as you would a younger child, know it's not purposeful.	Use parts language, animal stories with parts, wrapping all parts into self; praise for truth telling; Be firm with expressing displeasure at the behavior and offer positive sensory connection ASAP. Act as if the child is 3 to 4.

Responses to Specific Behaviors

Troubling Behavior	Step/Age Where Behavior is Usual	Age Where Behavior is Problematic	Child's Unmet Need
Stealing (takes anything)	3 to 24 months; preschoolers; heightened in early elementary years.	When excessive or at older ages. (in a teen look for drug problems)	Object permanence; severe deficit in permanence; child can't resist impulses; desperate to maintain connections.
Bowel and Bladder control	Infancy, toddler; nighttime bladder can occur until late elementary if muscle is weak or underdeveloped.	Older elementary; excessive; thought to be "deliberate" during the day.	Self permanence; cannot feel as if she exists if she can not smell, hear or feel herself. Safety from sexual abuse. Deep sleep or afraid to leave bedroom at night.
Compulsive Repetitive Behavior	0 to 18 months and again at 3-4 years; situational or when learning a new task.	Older child or if excessive.	Object Permanence; stability; attempting to "hold" self together to feel safe by repetition.
Running Away	18-30 months; shadowing and darting; 4 years; again at 6 –8years; early adolescence or when feeling unsafe.	Anytime.	Permanence; needs to be able to move away from parents and know that they and their love still exist. Parental inconstancy equals lost nurturing. She fears angry parent. She also feels that if I am too close I lose me and become you. I have no self-constancy.

Parent's Usual Response and Feelings	Parent's New Response	Treatment Interventions
Very upset, If personal property taken feels violated, frustrated; and betrayed; sees behavior as deliberate; hopeless; jumps ahead to predict jail time; untrusting; dislikes the child.	Understands that it's not deliberate; reacts as you would with a younger child; remove and or return the object; enforces rules and praises for giving back.	Use transitional objects (give the child things of yours that remind the child of you and your love, things that look, feel and smell like you); Play peek eye; hide and seek and find; turtle work; predict success. Act as if the child is 10 months to 3 years old.
Embarrassment; disgust; feels it's deliberate; very angry; wants to disown child; hopeless; worn out and tired.	Don't make it a huge focus – treat as you would younger child; don't reject or disown child, gently and firmly help child clean up.	Inside-outside; sensory aids (objects) to hold self as structure builds; fog body position then symbiotic position and games. Lot of peek-a-boo and hide and seek. "And you are still you!" Remember; respond as if the child is younger and not yet potty trained. Leave lights on. Maybe use a sensor alarm.
Drives parents crazy; annoyance; irritation; nagging; confused and powerless.	Patience; look for positives to praise.	Tell child "you can do that again, and then you stop and you are still you. Can you find your stopping part?" Freeze tag; musical chairs; hanky game all practice stopping.
Fear; anger; yelling; powerlessness; evokes desire to reject back.	Still fearful but understands the child isn't rejecting parent; calm, consistent, reassuring response.	Hide and seek; you are still you; shadow and dart; dance. Sports games of movement away from and back towards parents. Parts language. Permanence running is shorter and less angry; respond as if the child was a toddler. Provide constancy. Respond as if 3 – 5 year old child.

Responses to Specific Behaviors

Troubling Behavior	Step/Age Where Behavior is Usual	Age Where Behavior is Problematic	Child's Unmet Need
Cutting, picking or self mutilation	Not usual	Can present as self stimulation in neglected infants and toddlers	This demonstrates n lack of self permanence
Physical aggression, biting, scratching, hitting	11 months to 4 years (temper tantrums).	Older, excessive or violent.	Lack of permanence = rage. You are disappearing or I am disappearing. Lack of constancy = no impulse control, I am 100% what I am experiencing in the moment so denying the impulse is losing yourself.
Fire Starting	Fascination with light and power in infancy and toddler; playing with matches is normal and dangerous at 4 –8 years.	Older ages.	Permanence, extreme fog deficit; no trust or safety; no warmth or comfort; felt pain, degradation and violation with powerlessness. Shows rage.
Lack of Remorse	0 – 12 months; preschoolers sometimes; 4 –8 years occasionally; true remorse not possible until mid elementary years	Older	Lack of permanence = rage at lack of feeling the safety of a permanent existence. The child has no capacity yet for reciprocity. Child must have permanence to feel remorse and must equate to his own behavior—empathy.

Parent's Usual Response and Feelings	Parent's New Response	Treatment Interventions
They are afraid, scold the child or toll her to stop. Can't understand why a person would hurt herself.	Calmly tell the child he's safe, soothingly stop the behavior. Use the child's name to prove the child's existence. See a professional.	Work on permanence, transitional objects, child proof the house, lock up dangerous objects.
Mortified and frightened; embarrassed; angry.	Stay calm; contain behavior; comfort; tell the child you will help him until he can manage; if hurtful get professional help.	Work on permanency and constancy; give support in developing control. Set firm limits and let the child know it is not okay use his hitting part when angry. Help him connect with the nurturing part of you, think younger child!
Fear, frustration; feeling powerless and unsafe in their own home; feeling need to choose other children over this one; protection issue, tense.	Concern, plan for safety; seek professional help; believe that this too can be addressed.	Safety first; childproof house and environment; continue positive interactions; fog and symbiosis exercises; warmth and joy; stability.
Fear; feel like a failure; jump ahead to predict "jail time'; extreme dislike and disgust; rigid reaction	Don't borrow trouble; stay calm; be consistent and persistent; seek professional help	Use parts language and games; hokey-pokey; objects; here and there, up and down; symbiosis position and games. Teach apologies as you would to a toddler, using joined learning techniques

Section VI. Conclusion – The Dance Continues

All children, no matter whether adopted, foster or biological face multiple challenges while growing up. However, adopted and foster children can face additional hurtles. First, adoptive/foster parents don't always know the effect of the child's genetics; second, prenatal care or use of chemicals can cause brain damage; and third, early neglect or abuse seriously harms children psychologically. Because of this, adopted kids often miss early developmental steps. Science tells us that all steps need to be processed for the child's healthy emotional development.

The dance steps for establishing permanence and constancy are common and basic. The process seems simple, but it is also amazingly effective when made a priority. It only takes a small amount of time—perhaps 20 minutes a day—to enhance your child's life. It also means seizing opportunities when they arise—for instance time alone in a car ride to give praise or reinforce positive behaviors. Remember, it takes many many repetitions of these recommended interactions to build your child's capacity to have and to hold an attachment.

One 11 year-old girl, adopted at age nine after suffering years of neglect and abuse, recently gave her mom a bouquet of garden flowers with a note that said:

> Flowers are red,
> violets are blue,
> you are so caring,
> I love you too.

This was a very loving act—more typical of a six or seven year old—but wonderful none-the-less. When she first came home, she was very angry and unattached. After three and one-half years of work, revisiting in very creative ways earlier steps, she now sees herself as a multi-faceted person who is basically a "good girl" who has bad days. She no longer steals, seldom goes into rages, and shows her loving part on a regular basis. She has a chance at growing up and having a productive life.

As parents, we can't protect against every danger our children face—but we try. The wisdom contained in these pages will help you parent all of your children well—but is particularly helpful with challenging children.

Shining Spirit - by Mariah, age 13, a survivor

In my life
I see love
That love is in my spirit
sent from up above

God has given me a gift
my gift is a shining spirit
A spirit so very bright
that you think you can hear it

I'm an everyday person
but I stand out from the crowd
My heart wants to tell me
something
It's telling me something out loud

At first I was blinded
but now I can see
that I have a great power
that God has given me

As I grow older
my spirit will still shine
And it will flow forever
and it will always be mine

Section VII. Glossary

Attachment The child's bond with caregivers that grows through the child's experience of stable, reliable, consistent, safe, secure, comfortable, and loving care.

Attachment Formation This is the developmental process a child must complete to form effective attachments.

Belonging/Claiming Belonging is the experiential belief that membership in the family or connectedness will continue even when others know the hidden parts. What is outside goes inside. If the parent accepts all of me, she claims me, then I can accept all of me too.

Boundaries Boundaries are healthy internal limits a person establishes to protect self. They come from limits first set by parents. If they are missing, people can become enmeshed/codependent or totally disengage from the other.

Consolidation of Individuation A relationship built by two whole people bonded by trust, positive interactions. They both have the capacity to "hold" the existence and constancy of the other.

Constancy Constancy means the child's ability to see the parent and therefore the internal self as whole across space, time, emotion and experience. As the child learns through experience that mom is the same mom whether she is nurturing or angry, so the child learns that he too is the same whether angry or affectionate.

Discipline Discipline means to learn to control ones self in different environments and in different circumstances and to do what's right. Healthy discipline is not the same as control or punishment, but is rather a way to help the child to build self-discipline.

Differentiation The stage where the infant begins to discover that self and mother may not be one and the same. Differentiation to consolidation is often traditionally considered the birth of the separate self.

Evocative Permanence Evocative permanence refers to the loss of sensory contact with a person or thing that is important, something that evokes strong feelings or emotions. Evocative permanence means knowing the object or person that is important or that evokes strong feelings continuous to exist over time and space.

Fog The sensory stage immediately after birth when the child and parents are getting to know each other and building safety.

Funneling This technique helps guide or channel behavior. It works to help the child revisit the symbiotic stage—learning dependency on only one or two parents. You funnel by not letting the child be held, fed, or comforted by anyone other than parents for a significant period of time.

Holding Behaviors In beginning symbiosis, the infant cannot distinguish between himself and the parent. It is crucial that parents cradle the infant's body, pat the infant's back, gaze into the infant's eyes and rock the infant. Crucial behaviors that promote the sense of safety and security are essential to brain growth and attachment.

Homeostasis This is a feeling of balance. All living things seek to maintain a constant internal environment; it means a relatively stable state of equilibrium.

Intimate Eye Contact Symbiosis between an infant and parent usually begins with the first interactive smile. One of the features of the first interactive smile is the intimate (not forced) eye-to-eye contact that accompanies the exchange of smile. Eye contact is important for attachment to develop. (The eyes are the pathway to the soul.) Never force eye contact and remember that sight impaired people can and do form healthy attachment.

Joined Learning Joined learning is the spontaneous, encouraging, playful and nurturing way we teach toddlers facts, skills and feeling states. Joined learning is doing the task for the child, while encouraging the child to join in. Joined learning is helping the child find the answer, with encouragement and joy.

Object Constancy This is the understanding that objects and people don't simply disappear when out of sight. It also means the ability to use objects to "hold" the negative and positive parts of the self, to know that the angry self and the gentle self are different parts of the whole self.

Objects relations theory This theory hypothesizes that people develop their sense of themselves in

117

the world, through their experiences (and their perceptions of those experiences) with their primary caregivers.

Parts of self   An individual is made up of many physical and emotion elements or parts, i.e. happy, sad, creative, old, blond, angry, musical and more. Parts can also be hobbies, talents, or interests. A well-adjusted person learns that one type of behavior or feeling does not define the whole person. Children who have constancy problems believe themselves to be <u>all</u> mad and worthless when acting mad. Using the parts language—for example referring to the mad part—helps the child understand that his positive parts still exist and are accessible even when he's mad.

Permeability   This is the capacity to tell the difference between the self and the parent. The child begins to decide what emotions/feelings to let in and what to keep out. A person who doesn't have a secure sense of self can let in another—to be controlled or made to feel badly. A permeable parent may have difficulty telling the difference between the child's emotions and his own internal wounds,

Permanence   This   is   the individual's awareness that the parent and therefore the self, exists and will continue to exist across space, time, and emotion. Permanence is the capacity to know and to feel in a sensory—not cognitive way—that the parent continues to exist when out of actual contact.

Proprioception   The   sixth   sense, proprioception, refers to a combination of body position in space and the vestibular sense of movement and rhythm.

Rapprochement   Vacillation between practicing independence and seeking return to oneness is the hallmark of the rapprochement stage. Evocative object permanence is still fairly weak at this stage. A toddler in rapprochement can manage some experiences of separateness and falls apart in others. Teens typically re-experience the rapprochement stage.

Refueling   Babies and toddlers maintain their sense of connectedness by going to and away from caregivers. They gradually spend more and more time further away from their parents. The ability to "hold" the internal feeling of the parent's availability with just a visual check is still limited.

Representational permanence   This is the capacity to "remember" and "feel" as if items that are not important still exist when out of sensory contact.

Resiliency   A person is resilient when able to hold self-constancy—to know that no matter what life brings them, they will be the same, likeable, capable people. A sudden change in our lives can shake our sense of who we are. How quickly a person recovers is a sign of resilience.

Shadowing and Darting   This game allows the toddler to experience the power of moving away, be an independent self, operate under his own steam, coupled with the ability to draw the parent to him, to keep the connection. The toddler experiences self-induced momentary absence of the sensory presence (shadowing and catching) of the parent.

Stability Stability is the capacity to control and contain changing emotions most of the time and in most situations.

Symbiosis The earliest sense of intense, repetitive, positive interaction between parent and baby which causes them to fall in love. They behave as if one person, satisfying each other's needs. Symbiosis is a hallmark of romantic love.

Transitional objects These are objects such as blankets, teddies, pictures, or pacifiers that soothe a child's anxiety when "out of touch" with the caregiver. Transitional objects evoke sensory responses that evoke the baby's experience of safety, security, comfort, and warmth when the parent "holds" them. Transitional objects bridge the gap between dawning awareness that the source of security is the parent and the capacity to know that the parent continues to exist and is available when out of sensory contact.

Validation Validation is recognizing and accepting the other person's feelings. It doesn't mean that you agree with the person's feelings, but it does demonstrate that you hear and respect their point of view.